MEN
MONEY
FOOD

My Journey from Addiction to Joy!

DEBORAH COLLINS

Dedication

To my mother who left school and gave up her dream of becoming a ballerina to have me and raise me.

To my four-legged family who is always there for me with a wet nose and a kiss to cheer me up!

This book is for Alma, who helped me pick up the pieces after my divorce; Her calming nature soothed my soul.

Table of Contents

Acknowledgements

I would like to thank Dorothy "The Organizer" Breininger, star of the hit TV show *Hoarders* and Author of *Stuff Your Face or Face your Stuff, Lose Weight by Decluttering Your Life*, who has helped me organize not only my life, but my mind, when trying to put my thoughts down on paper for this book.

I would like to thank Pamela DeNeuve, Author of *The Handbook for Healing* for always encouraging me and never giving up on me. My original life coach, she and I go way back and she knows where all of the darkness lies. Her wisdom and expertise helped me see my 'blind spots' and turn on the light.

A huge thank you to Deb Richards, Author of *Shift and Shine*, for her unending support and friendship. She and I have shared much pain and joy, and gratefully came through the other side victorious!

I want to thank my dear friend Anne Monaghan for her careful attention to detail, and the hours she invested to listen and read and hone in on nuances of the message I was trying to impart.

Lastly, much gratitude to my core writing friends who believed in me: Elizabeth Moore Kraus, Sabrina La Vista, Katie Bradley, Stephanie Kraemer, Denice Girardeau, April Wyett, Lisa Kruckeberg, Cecile Higgins, Jan Huerta, TC Armstrong and Nadine M. They helped me learn persistence and structure.

Preface

I come from a long history of "not getting it right;" making bad choices, sabotaging myself, wishing that I could do it over.

I get so many opportunities…the universe wants to help, but I keep impeding its attempts.

I'm an only child who had the feeling that my father did not love me. The theme my mother tried to convey is, "He loves you … he just doesn't know how to show it." Oh, poor him. My other friends' moms seemed to be able to find men that did, in fact, "know how to show it."

I've been on a quest all my life to find one of those.

The list of relationships I've had is a long one. With each new relationship, I tried to find the one that would prove his love for me and not leave. In looking for that, I believe I've settled for underachievers (broken birds) or I've spent my time pushing qualified men away in an attempt to make them prove their undying love for me. If I was a bitch and tried to push them away and they didn't go, they must love me …

But I'm getting ahead of myself.

CHAPTER 1

How it Began

"**G**OD DAMN IT ... LOOK WHAT YOU'VE DONE NOW!"

It was a hot summer day when I was jolted from my afternoon nap by my enraged father shaking me.

"Look at this mess!" he shouted, face red and screaming, his hot breath on my face. I was so confused that I bit my tongue and began to cry.

What's happening? I thought.

"Daddy, what's wrong?" I asked, but before the words were out of my mouth my father threw the sheets off of me, pulled me from my bed, and began to smack me on my behind.

"You – went – to – bed – with – candy!" he yelled the words between each blow to my butt and bare legs.

I was four years old and along with my favorite naptime Snoopy dog, had gone to bed with my PEZ candy dispenser. My bed was against the wall under an open window and while I slept, an army of ants, looking for water and relief from the heat, had marched up the side of the house through the open window and into my bed.

In that moment of utter terror, I fixed my gaze on the steady stream of ants on the wall, and asked myself, *Daddy, why do you hate me?*

Overreaction and drama are a big part of my story and can be traced to the role my father played as my primary caretaker. Mom worked days, so this meant I was left with a man who hated much of everything, including his job, his life, and me.

Since he needed an easy target on which to land his frustrations, he picked me.

At an early age, I got the message that something was wrong with me. That I was defective. That everything was my fault.

But even then, I was a survivor, and was able to figure out what I needed to do to endure him: Be a good girl. Don't make any waves. Fit In. Assimilate.

I became a chameleon and a people pleaser.

I grew up the daughter of a cop and a secretary. We lived modestly, yet had everything we needed. My mother, Marvel, worked two jobs. An executive secretary by day, she took in ironing at night for extra income, which provided my father with what he wanted—his "toys"— and not to be burdened by the extra expense that was me.

I was seven and it was Christmas—my favorite holiday. My mom went all out with the decorations. We always had plenty of gifts piled up under a beautiful tree. The tree would be one we picked as a family. We made an afternoon of it, going to the local tree lot on the corner and finding the perfect one.

I remember one year, when I found the tree I wanted. My dad told the young boy working there, "We'll take this one." Mom and I watched as a scrawny kid, who had been hired to handle the largest of trees, dragged it to our car and tied it to the top of Mom's orange Bel Air Chevy so that we could get it home.

Dad unloaded the tree and took it inside while Mom and I scurried to make room. We filled the red metal stand with water, as he carefully set the huge tree in the container and tightened the three screws to hold it in place. Mom carefully placed the embroidered skirt that my grandmother had made around the bottom.

Then, with Nat King Cole crooning Christmas music from the record player, we all began to decorate it. The living room had a delicious smell of pine and salty popcorn, which my mom had prepared to string on the tree. Usually, we ate more than we strung. It was a wonderful afternoon, laughing, singing, and placing garlands strand by strand for the final effect. I loved these moments when the family was close and happy.

It was finally Christmas morning and our house had that freshly cut tree smell that made me love this holiday.

I couldn't wait to see what Santa had brought me. I had strict orders to stay in my room until one of my parents came to get me.

Did Santa come last night? I wondered.

"Moooomm," I would wail impatiently. "Hurry up!"

I could not wait to open presents. Finally, I heard the door to my parents' bedroom open right across the hall from me.

"Merry Christmas," my mom said, kissing me, her hair askew and pointing in many directions. "Just a little longer, honey," she said as she headed down the hall to the kitchen. "We just need to wait for your dad."

She closed my door and I could hear her making coffee. I busied myself with my sketch pad, and after what seemed an eternity, I heard the words, "Come on out." I ran down the hall full of anticipation. I stopped in front of the tree, my eyes as wide as the smile on my face. Christmas morning was always magic to me.

In front of me was a fully assembled Barbie dollhouse complete with furnishings, supposedly left by Santa. I could not believe my eyes. As I stood there transfixed, my eyes landed next on a beautiful pink Schwinn bicycle with a white banana seat and big wide chrome handlebars that had pink and white streamers coming out of them.

"I love it!" I shrieked, as I jumped up and down. "Can I go ride it?"

"After breakfast," Mom laughed, pulling the cinnamon rolls out of the oven. Christmas mornings were wonderful.

Everyone was happy.

My father's parents were visiting this Christmas. My grandmother liked to come to Las Vegas to gamble. She loved the slots. My father's parents were German. They didn't talk much and the word that best describes them is *stern*.

As I rummaged under the tree looking for another present, I found a large box that said "Debbie" on it. The tag read, "From G & G."

"Thank you," I said, as I carried the large box carefully back to the section on the floor where I was camped out with my gifts, torn wrapping paper, and ribbons all around me. *What could this be?* I wondered as I quickly tore the paper off. Another horse statue for my collection? A book? Roller skates? Once the paper was removed, I saw a plain brown box with a lid. I removed the lid and looked into the box, not understanding what I was looking at. I reached in and pulled out a large, heavy object, and cocked my head to the side quizzically.

"I made it in ceramics class," my grandmother said. "I hope you like it."

"Uh, thanks," I muttered quietly, looking down. The gift was a bunch of purple resin grapes that used to be popular in the '60s. I hid my disappointment the best I could and stared at my mother. She looked at me and shrugged, and I could see the pain on her face. It would be years before I found out why.

After all of the presents were opened, crumpled

wrapping paper strewn everywhere, my mom was in the kitchen slamming cupboards—the magical Christmas spell was broken like a bar at 2 am when the lights came on and all that's left was the empty bottles and the over-full ashtrays. We were now in work mode, getting the preparations going for the holiday meal.

My favorite Christmas was when I was nine. My cousin Jeff had come to live with us, and he became the brother I'd always wanted. We each got a transistor radio and a microphone. I wanted to be a famous singer. Jeff and I donned the Beatle wigs we'd received as gifts and together began to sing, "She loves you ya ya ya…and with a love like that…"

Jeff and I were inseparable. His mother, my mom's sister, rarely visited, and I didn't know her very well, but one day she showed up with Jeff in tow, stayed a few hours, and left without him. I overheard my mom telling my dad that my aunt was dating a new man and raising her son would get in the way of him marrying her, so she asked my parents if we could take him in. He became my best friend and brother and brought out my fun side. But Jeff also had a dark side. His parent's divorce at such an early age caused him so much pain. His father was no longer in the picture. I was too young to understand his sadness when he went off by himself, lost, deep in his thoughts. He wasn't with us long because he started using drugs and my dad would not tolerate it. He was 17 and was sent off to the military and I never saw him again. Unfortunately, he continued to use drugs there and had an accidental overdose. His death left a hole in all our hearts.

Though my early memories with my father were difficult, it seemed that Christmas brought a different feeling into the house. The weight of the rest of the year seemed to disappear for at least a few days and we felt like a normal and happy family.

CHAPTER 2

Alone and Lonely

My mom had me out of wedlock in the 1950s, and in those days, she was branded with a red letter "A" on her chest, and thus began her life of apologizing for her existence. She felt ashamed and she passed that shame onto me.

Part of her penance for finding a man to marry her was to be-all and do-all for him. So, when she wasn't working, she was catering to her man, which left me alone and lonely. As a result, I became good at isolating and occupying myself.

"Leave the door open," I would call out to Mom as she was leaving my room after kissing me and saying good night. I was afraid of the dark.

"Of course, honey," she would reassure while leaving the door ajar and the hall light on. However, if my father was the one on bedtime duty, I would be left in the dark with a "Grow up!" as he harshly closed the door. Ron was less than nurturing.

* * * * *

I was about 10 when I began having a recurring dream of a beautiful white Victorian house in a rural area that I didn't recognize. As I stood outside under the shade of a large weeping willow tree looking up at the house's second-floor window, I watched as a piece of paper gently fell out of the sky and slowly floated down to the ground at my feet. I bent down and picked up the crinkled paper. My small fingers smoothed it open, and I could see a name that was different from mine. I was aware that there was a message being given, but I was too young to know what it was. Each time I would wake up with a start—upset and confused. Looking back on this dream later in my life, I realized my subconscious mind was letting me know something that my parents had not said. My father was not mine. Maybe on some level, I knew. Perhaps I had overheard a family member talking about it, or found some papers in my parents' desk when I was rummaging through their office.

One morning when I was 12 years old, I confronted my parents at the dining room table.

"Am I adopted?" I asked accusingly.

"Don't be ridiculous," my father answered sharply. My

mother was silent as she put the scrambled eggs in front of me. They gave no other explanation.

Satisfied and relieved, I let it go. I took their answer at face value and believed them. Of course, that was the answer I wanted to hear. This would not be the first time I practiced "magical thinking."

* * * * *

Life wasn't all bad, and most of the time, I felt like a typical kid.

One Saturday, I was lying on the grass staring up at the clouds, my beautiful black standard poodle, Sunshine, beside me. I loved to make formations out of the clouds and had just found an Indian Chief riding a horse.

A tomboy, I was happiest at home playing with my lizards and horny toads or dressing up Sunshine and hanging out in my room.

"Hey, let's go," my dad said coming from the garage, keys in hand, heading for the truck. Sunshine and I quickly ran to him, and jumped into the cab of the blue Chevy pickup and we took off toward the billowing black cloud in the distance. My dad loved to chase fires, and if it was the weekend, he took me with him. It was always a fun adventure.

"Take the wheel," Dad said once we got out of the city, arching his back, and reaching for something as I steered, concentrating on the road. He pulled the short black comb out of the back pocket of his jeans, grabbed a gas receipt from the glovebox, folded it horizontally, and placed it over the comb. Then he put the comb to his mouth and started to blow. Funny sounds came out and I started to laugh as my dad started singing the popular Willie Nelson song, "On the Road Again," on his homemade kazoo.

"Just can't wait to get on the road again," I joined in. These were the special moments that I loved when I had him to myself and I felt close to him. These moments were rare.

As an only child, often on my own, I had to learn how to entertain myself, and one of my favorite ways was to read. I was a bookworm and could lose myself in a Nancy Drew mystery or a book about horses for hours. I also loved to draw and sketch. Although I was quiet and liked to stay inside, my mother, on the other hand, was very active and tried to draw me out.

"Get your nose out of that book and come and play," she chided.

She was very popular with all of the neighborhood kids. She loved to run and play and often engaged them in water balloon fights. They loved her.

"I'm reading," I'd say without looking up. This would generally invoke a barrage of shaming comments or mocking tones. It was a constant battle between us.

* * * * *

The three of us would often take weekend trips to our cabin in St. George, Utah, a few hours from home. This is where I discovered horses, and I loved the times my parents and I would ride for hours through the woods.

After begging my mom for riding lessons, she finally agreed. She drove me every Saturday for a year to Willow Springs Ranch for my weekly lessons so that I could ride in the parade. My room was full of ribbons and bronze horse statues. I was obsessed.

In the late '60s, Las Vegas was still a predominantly western town, and the city made a big deal of the annual Helldorado Parade, rodeo, and carnival. This year was no different, and I was looking forward to it.

Smiling at my reflection in the full-length mirror in my room, I liked what I saw: a slim girl with straight blond hair in tight red riding pants and a white cotton shirt with ruffles. I finished off the look with a white cowboy hat, white cowboy boots, and a thin white belt with a big silver buckle on it.

"I'm ready, Mom," I said, and we headed out the door.

"I'm sorry I can't stay to watch," Mom said, pulling into the fairgrounds parking lot.

"I have to get that ironing delivered."

"I know, Mom—it's ok," I said, my eyes scanning the rows of horse trailers, looking for my group. Locating them, I leaned over and kissed her.

"Thanks, Mom," I said, running toward my horse to get saddled up.

"I love you. Be careful," she called out before the door slammed.

My mare Ki Ki and I were a wonderful team and we carried our Nevada Silver State flag with pride.

* * * * *

One weekend after the parade, we were headed to our cabin in Utah. My parents had been joined by their close friends, Bud and Glory, and their son David. David was a senior in high school, which made him four years older than me. With the adults up front in the truck, he and I were relegated to riding in the bed of the truck on the three-hour drive to the mountains. David and I were huddled close with the blankets pulled up tight around our necks.

"Brrrrr," David said. "Why don't you get closer and keep me warm?" he inched over my way.

What a dweeb, I thought to myself. But it was so cold I had no choice but to stay under the blanket next to him. David was pushy and irritating. Before long, he was making unwanted passes at me and kept grabbing me under the bedding.

"Stoopp," I hissed, "or I will tell my father!"

David, seeing this as a huge game, was relentless. I'd had enough! I reached up behind me and rapped on the truck window. Dad pulled the truck over. I was scared and relieved at the same time.

"He's touching me," I said.

"She's crazy," David said.

All my dad said was, "Knock it off," and got back in the truck and drove off. The parents up front were oblivious to the terror their son was causing this defenseless tween in the back of the truck.

* * * * *

I discovered boys a couple of years later when I was about 13. My diary is full of entries about this boy or that one. None of these crushes lasted long and they were just fantasy romances that filled my mind and my heart. My quest to be loved began at an early age.

My parents used Sundays as their romance/reconnect day. They would send me off to the local Lutheran church by myself so that they could have their alone time. I was the designated parishioner of the family. The pious placeholder with the responsibility to make the family look good. I didn't really mind. I loved being at church and even sang in the choir.

One day as I was walking to church, head down, the wind blowing my Sunday dress all around me, a car pulled up with a tall, good-looking young man behind the wheel, with his tan arm resting on the open window.

"Where are you going?" he asked, smiling.

"Church," I said, sweeping the hair out of my eyes and continuing to walk.

"Want a ride?" he offered.

"No," I said, trying to keep my dress from blowing around my head, as I kept moving forward. The old red Mustang continued to drive slowly at my side while I walked, and he told me his name was Mike. He asked mine. We talked the rest of the way to church. Mike asked if he could see me after church, and I invited him to my house that afternoon. I was 15 and not allowed to date but could invite boys to the house if my parents were home. Mike was 18 and had just graduated high school.

"Come on in," I said, opening the door. Mike walked in hesitantly and looked around, noticing my dad strategically parked in the living room, cleaning his gun.

"Dad, this is Mike," I said.

"Hi, Mike, nice to meet you," my dad said and pretended to be absorbed in his task.

"Uh, let's go outside," I said and quickly guided him to the backyard by the pool.

"Leave it open," my dad called out, referring to the sliding glass door. Making sure he was in our line of sight, my dad made a point to look menacing as he reassembled the rifle and cocked it several times loudly in our direction.

I was entranced with Mike's dark good looks. I didn't know anything about him, but I was loving the attention. I don't recall our conversation exactly, but I have a very clear memory of what happened like it was yesterday.

Dee Dee and I were best friends. She was blond, petite, and a little wild. She would come to my house after school. My parents worked, so we had the house to ourselves. One day after school, Mike came over with his friend and took Dee Dee and me to his house. Once there, we paired off.

"Come with me." Mike took my hand and led me down the hallway to his room, showing me rows of trophies that he had won playing baseball. I did not know he was an athlete. I didn't know anything about him. I just knew he liked me and I was flattered.

"I like your room," I said nervously, making small talk.

"Thanks," Mike said as he casually walked over, locked the door, and returned to the bed where I was sitting. He pushed me back on the twin bed with the plaid bedspread and began to kiss me. I was new at this and trying not to be nervous.

We were making out when Dee Dee knocked and said, "Deb, we gotta go—it's 4 o'clock."

I started to get up, but Mike held me down and said tensely to the door, "We'll be out in a minute."

"I need to go," I said, struggling to get up.

Mike tightened his grip on my neck, pushed me back, and as I continued to squirm he pulled out a knife, which he switched open and held to my throat, and said, "If you make a sound, I will use this."

He pulled down my pants with his foot and jammed himself roughly into me. I could not move, frozen with fear. *What was I doing here?* I thought, beginning to panic! The pain when he penetrated me was like a searing bolt of fire. There was nothing romantic about it. He forced himself on me with no foreplay—no emotion. I was shocked and stunned by what had just happened.

He'd raped me.

When he was done, he hissed in my ear,

"If you tell anyone, I will kill you—I know where you live and I will kill you and your family."

With that, he stood up, pulled up his pants, raked his fingers through his hair, and said, "Let's go."

I got off the bed in a daze and smoothed my clothes, my innocence shattered forever. I left that room and I left that house and told no one. Not Dee Dee, not my parents, not my dog, or my diary. From that point forward, I shut off my feelings and pretended it didn't happen.

Some months passed. One evening, I was home with my parents. We'd just sat down to dinner when the phone rang. I picked up the orange phone on the wall with the long cord.

"Hello?" I said.

"Remember what I told you," the familiar voice said, and the line went dead in my hand.

"Who was it?" my dad asked.

"Wrong number," I answered and grabbed a slice of pepperoni pizza to stuff down the fear and shame that I felt and proceeded to carry with me for years to come.

CHAPTER 3

The Unraveling

Not long after the rape, my life began to unravel. While many adolescent girls were getting ready for prom and excitedly making plans for their future, I was isolating and shutting down. My parents began to fight a lot.

My mom loved to tease and joke around; serious emotion was not her thing. One day, she and her friend Barbara were sitting in our dining room. As I walked to the fridge to get a drink, I heard Barbara say, "Seriously, Marvel, we can do it. You'd make a stunning blond."

My mom, a dark brunette, laughed. "Well, blonds do have more fun I hear."

"I have an extra box of L'Oreal Preference in my car," my mom's platinum-blond friend said. "Let me get it."

When she returned, the friends giggled and went into

the kitchen to whip up the concoction that would transform my mom and put some pep in her step. After waiting the prescribed amount of time, my mom leaned far over the sink as Barbara removed the excess hair dye and wrapped her head in a towel. Anxiously my mom ran to the mirror hanging in the living room and removed the towel.

"Shit, it's orange!" she cried.

"Oh no," Barbara replied. "Don't panic, we just have to put a toner on it."

Luckily, Barbara was a hairdresser, so she went out to her car for more product and quickly whipped up a new batch. This happened three more times that day until it was finally right. *Who was this platinum-blond bombshell in our kitchen and what had she done with my mother?* I thought.

"OH MY GOD, OHHH MYYY GOD!" my mom kept repeating. "Ron is gonna kill me."

The two giggled some more and Barbara took her leave.

"Let me know how it goes," she shot over her shoulder as she left the house.

"Okay, wish me luck," my mom responded and went into her room and put on her makeup to complete the transformation. At 6 pm, we heard Dad's truck pull into the driveway. Mom came into the hallway looking beautiful and stood at the door.

Before she opened it, she said to me, "Let's surprise him," and flattened herself against the wall.

My dad walked into the house and at first, he only saw me.

"Hi, where's your mother?" His common refrain.

"Oh, she's around," I said mysteriously, my mom hiding behind the door, hearing it all.

"Hey, hon," he called out. "I'm home."

My mom jumped out from behind the door.

"Surprise!" she said, laughing.

Ron's mouth fell open, but he was not smiling.

"How do you like it?" she asked. This project had taken all day for my mom and Barbara to complete and my dad was pissed.

"What did you do?" he said.

"Don't you like it?" my mom shot back.

"No, I hate it—you look cheap."

They continued this conversation down the hallway and into their bedroom where they slammed the door, but it wasn't necessary because I could still hear everything. I went into my room and tried to bury my ears in my dog's neck so that I couldn't hear. Before long, the bedroom door opened and my father stormed down the hall. I heard the front door slam and the truck engine rev loudly and peel out from the drive. Hours passed and my mom was quiet, trying to act as though nothing was going on. Later that night, she locked the front door and told me it was time for bed.

"Okay, Mom," I said, sad for her. "Goodnight. I think you look pretty."

"Thanks, honey," she said and smiled wearily.

Not long after I'd gone to bed, I heard shouting and pounding on the door. I ran down the hallway to the front door and saw my mom attempting to keep my dad outside.

"Help me!" mom implored, and together we used all our strength to push the door closed. We both knew what would follow when my father was in this enraged state. He had used his key, but the door still wouldn't open, because mom had bolted it from the inside. Frustrated, my dad smashed his fist through the window on the entrance door and glass flew everywhere.

"Shit," he said, and we saw the blood where the jagged glass had cut his arm when he reached through the window.

"Just go!" my mom said, "or I will call Seymour."

Seymour was my uncle, a judge in town who they both respected, and who often acted as their mediator and marriage counselor. With that, my dad finally got tired of trying and left on his own. This was one of many fights that started as nothing and escalated to being so loud and violent.

"Go to bed, honey," my mom said, squatting down to pick up the glass.

* * * * *

Not long after the divorce, my mother packed me up and moved us to San Diego, where I attended my junior year of high school. My mother worked hard to brush up on her typing and shorthand skills, and before long, she landed a job as an executive secretary.

One day after a long day of school, not wanting to go home to an empty house, I drove to visit my mom's friend who lived nearby. I entered the small, neat home on a quiet street and got a big hug from the woman who'd been introduced to me as Beverly, my mom's childhood bestie.

"Come in, honey," she said, hugging me. "How was your day?"

"It was okay," I said, enjoying the smell of the popcorn that she was making.

Three of her kids, who were around my age, were sprawled on the floor of the cozy living room watching TV and two were looking at a photo album.

"Hey, Deb, check this out," said Bobby, the oldest. I got on the floor with him and his sister, kneeling to see the photo better.

"That's your dad," Bobby said, turning his head to look at me.

Squatting next to him, I looked over his shoulder at the picture of the heavy-set, smiling bald man, and said, "That's not my dad."

"Yes, it is," he said. "I overheard my dad talking about it. You and I are cousins!"

Blinded by the shock of what I'd heard, I ran out of the house, fumbled for my keys, got in my car, and just drove, not caring where. Finally stopping at the beach, I sat staring out at the ocean from the parking lot and thought,

No wonder my father and his parents did not love me.

I was not their blood.

Confused and lost, I kept this secret for some time, telling no one. Not even my mom.

We'd been in San Diego for six months. I was 17 and had finally adjusted to San Diego and the new school. It was a hot Saturday afternoon and I was visiting my grandmother who lived nearby. I was in the backyard tanning in a chaise lounge when the gardeners came. Before long I noticed one of the workers. He looked like the poster of Jim Morrison that I had over my bed back home. He was tall, lean, and tan. His golden-brown hair reached his shoulders and he was shirtless. He looked like a god to me. My eyes never left him that day and the following week when he came by to do the lawn, I made sure to be there.

"Hi," he said. "I'm Tim."

"I'm Debbie," I said, blushing.

His tanned chest was bare and I could barely make eye contact with him. He told me that he was staying with his stepdad and helping him with his lawn business. I was smitten. We became an item and I forgot all about the pain of leaving Las Vegas. From that day forward, Tim and I were inseparable. It had been two years since I'd been raped, and I'd had no other sex since that time. We'd decided that we were going to have sex. I skipped school and went to his house. He handed me a bottle of Boone's Farm wine and told me to chug it down, which I did. It was a rainy day and we lay in each other's arms and professed our forever love. This was nothing like the brusque, cold, painful experience that I'd had with Mike.

Tim and I continued to meet at his house when we could. Unfortunately, one day soon after, his stepfather saw my car outside his house, which was not where I was supposed to be. He walked in unannounced and saw us having sex. I was sitting upright on top of Tim, fully exposed. I was so scared and ashamed. I quickly dressed and left. News must have traveled fast because, by the time I got home, my mother was waiting for me, hands on hips.

"You had sex with that boy?!"

"So what—" came my belligerent reply, "You did it too when you were my age!"

She looked at me wide-eyed and sat down wearily on the bed. She had no idea that I knew that she had gotten pregnant at 17, and that the man I called my father was actually my stepfather. She began to cry, defeated. She reached out her hand to me and I sat beside her as the whole story poured out of her. She explained that Ron would not let her tell me that he was not my father, because he thought I wouldn't love him if I knew. She'd been hiding this secret all these years. She explained how she'd gotten pregnant and was kicked out of school and her home all at the age of 17. Her parents disowned her, she never graduated, and she gave up all of her dreams. For me.

Pregnant with me and unsure of her future, my mom had moved to San Francisco to stay with her best friend

Beverly, the woman I'd recently met, now living in San Diego. Beverly gave my mom a roof, and a bed, and supported her while she got on her feet.

Beverly was my mom's childhood friend and had married the brother of my biological father, so she was technically my aunt. Mom explained that I'd actually had three father figures in my life all before I was three years old. There was Jack, the biological one; Dwayne, the second one, meant to make me legitimate; and then there was Ron, the cop, who would become my father for the next 16 years. Each one of these men left. In the naive mind of a little girl, I took their departure to be my fault. I could not get them to stay. Thus began my pattern of pushing men away before the inevitable happened and they left.

We left San Diego shortly after that. Mom didn't trust me with Tim and she could not handle the stress of life alone without Ron. We moved back to Las Vegas and began again. I needed to complete my senior year of high school and then I'd be done. Once back in my hometown, I reconnected with my old friends and became immersed in school and working. I was busy, and I was happy. But now Ron, my stepfather, was back in the picture. We still had a very contentious relationship, but I wanted my mom to be happy and he seemed to be on his best behavior with her. Despite this, I was still stunned and heartbroken to learn that the only father I had known wasn't my dad. My world was shattered. So often, growing up, I had heard people comment on how much I looked like him. I saw it, too: the same skin tone, the same deep-set eyes, the light brown hair color and texture. I was his little girl.

Who am I now? I thought. *Where do I belong*? I had lost my identity and my world was spinning out of control.

My father and I never spoke of this truth that had been uncovered. There was no explanation from him about why he felt it best to keep this important information from me. Our relationship did not have that transparency or trust. It was the elephant in the room that wasn't discussed.

Mom and Dad remarried, but it did not last long.

After the wedding, Ron moved into the house my mom and I had rented when we returned from San Diego. But now, with the knowledge that he was not my biological father, coupled with the years of his abuse and secrecy, this house was not big enough for the three of us to be under the same roof. He was back to his controlling ways.

It was a beautiful spring Saturday. My mom and I had been out shopping. We pulled into the driveway, gathered our bags, and entered the door to our little bungalow, laughing and at ease with each other. Noticing a scowling Ron in the middle of the living room, we stopped mid-sentence. He was holding up my gym bag and staring at my mother.

"What's up, honey?" my mom asked.

"This is what's up," he said excitedly, holding his hand out to my mom displaying the round plastic case of little pink pills like a trophy he had won. "Your daughter is on birth control!" he crowed, his eyes bulging.

"You went through my bag?" I asked incredulously. He had gone through my things while we were out and found my birth control pills which he showed to my mother, apparently evidence that I was a bad girl and not to be trusted. "Unbelievable," I said, stomping off to my room and slamming the door. I was so angry that my privacy had been violated. These pills were prescribed to me by my doctor to treat my acne. But they actually did have a dual purpose.

I was beginning to date older and more worldly men. David was one of these men. Overly pretty and very smooth, his mother was a famous country singer, and he had grown up in Las Vegas where she was a frequent headliner. He was a player. I liked to visit his apartment to use the swimming pool, and afterward, we would have sex. The one time he came to our house to meet my mother, he was overtly flirty with her and his actions let it be known that he was sleeping with me. He wore a gold pinky ring that he constantly played with while he talked to you. One side of the ring spelled out L O V E, the other F U C K.

"Check out my ring," David said to my mother, showing the "love" side up.

"Nice," my mom said. As she leaned in to take a look, David turned the ring, displaying the four-letter word on the other side.

"How about this," David leered at her.

My mom hit him with the towel she had in her hand and backed away.

"Rude!" my mom said flustered. The word that described him best is slimy. Nevertheless, I was drawn to him. Physically, he was not my type, but sexually, we were compatible. When my parents remarried, however, they made it clear that I was not to see him again, and since I was living under their roof, I complied.

Soon after the wedding, the three of us moved to a new house in a newer area of Las Vegas, but it was short-lived, and I moved out shortly thereafter.

The tension between me and Ron was causing problems between him and my mom, and it was decided that I needed to move out so that I could exercise my independence. I was 18, had graduated, and needed to go.

My mother and I set out on a bittersweet journey, scouring the streets with want ads in hand in search of an apartment and my imminent freedom. The weight of uncertainty hung between us as we explored the possibilities of a new chapter for me and the hopes that she had made the right decision in hers. We had been each other's life raft for the past two years and now we were both attempting to swim on our own to the new lives that awaited us.

Apartment after apartment, the towering complexes loomed over us, each promising a different future. But it was Lake Sahara, nestled in a tranquil oasis, that spoke to me and seemed like the perfect haven. A cozy studio, near the UNLV campus, with an affordable price tag of $800 per month, seemed well worth it, considering the promises of freedom it offered.

We paid the deposit and went home to pack.

My mother cried as we loaded my belongings into the trunk of my little green VW Bug.

Later, as my mom and I stepped inside the apartment, a feeling of excitement surrounded me. It was the first time I'd ever been away from the familiar comforts of home and the strict confines of being the daughter of a cop. The nervous flutter in my heart along with a sense of adventure told me this was my time to spread my wings.

After I said goodbye to my mother and closed the door behind her, I was alone. The space, though small, emanated a warmth that assuaged my fears. This apartment was all mine, a refuge where I could unravel the complexities of my identity and forge a path of my own.

But even in my newfound independence, the invisible thread connecting me to my mother remained unbroken. Each day, without fail, after my day ended, alone in the studio, I reached for the phone, dialing her number. I needed to tell her about my day. Whether it was a trivial matter or simply craving her familiar voice, our daily conversations bridged the physical distance between us.

In those moments, the distance evaporated, and it felt as if we were still navigating the world side by side. The bond between mother and daughter, unbreakable and eternal, kept us connected even as life propelled us forward in different directions.

And so, in that cozy studio apartment, amidst the city buzzing with bright lights 24 hours a day, I discovered the delicate balance between independence and the enduring need for connection.

"Hello," she said groggily.

"Mom, there's a spider in my room."

"Deb, it's 12:30 am, are you ok?"

"I just can't sleep!"

"Honey, take your shoe and hit it—I'll stay on the phone."

As I grabbed my shoe and squashed that bug, letting out a scream, I realized that she and I were very connected, and I still needed her close. She was all I had and she was my anchor. The spider in my bedroom, although small, served as a reminder that when there was a catastrophe, the comfort of a mother's love and support was only a phone call away.

CHAPTER 4

On My Own

One evening, not long after I moved into my new apartment, as I was putting away the last of the dinner dishes, I heard a knock at the door. I threw the dish towel over my shoulder, took a few steps to the foyer, opened the door, and stood facing my mother and her new boyfriend. They stood there looking like truant teenagers with a bottle of Dom Pérignon and matching sheepish grins.

"What a surprise," I said, scowling. This could not be good. "Come in," I said reluctantly.

Sitting across from them, I looked at my mother with this man. They were giddy.

"We've decided to move to Salt Lake City and get married," my mother explained.

They sat together holding hands, on my green velvet

couch, watching me expectantly. I was dumbstruck.

"What are you talking about?" I asked, not believing what I'd heard.

"It's a great opportunity," I heard the stranger say. "We can have a new beginning and get away from your crazy father."

My stepfather, Ron, although divorced from my mom and already with a new girlfriend, had begun to stalk my mom. Every time she would go out, she'd look over her shoulder, afraid he'd be in the bushes watching, ready to jump out and accost her at any time. She'd arrive home from a date and find telltale signs that he was near, like a broken cigarette on the hedge next to the door. It was a very frightening feeling knowing no one could help. She couldn't call the cops. He WAS the cops.

My mom had had enough. She was ready to move on. With this new guy, Richard. We called him Faaaaantaaastic. Any time you asked him how he was, he was faaaaantaaastic. He was a salesman. I never liked him much. They married and he brought two kids to the marriage. She was now a stepmom and still had to work, and they lived in an apartment with no furniture for a long while. He didn't do much to add to her world; she brought much more to his. They stayed married for seven years. There was a politeness between us, and I did grow to love his kids, but him...not so much. They began to drink heavily together, their answer to life's difficulties.

Now an adult, living on my own in a small apartment,

I needed to support myself. My mother had abandoned ship and my father had a new girlfriend. I did not know how to cope.

My first job after high school was working the counter at Montgomery Ward in the parts department. Now that I was on my own, I needed to make much more money to support myself. I tried various jobs; I worked for a short time at Hamilton Investments, a brokerage firm where I learned to sell commodities. The company traded futures and bet on whether the price of these items would go up or down. If the price went up, the client made money; if it went down, they didn't, and the investor had to make up the difference between the purchased price and the current price. It was pure speculation.

This was a straight commission job—each broker had to find their own leads and there was a quota each week of how much we had to sell. I was young, with very limited resources, so I reached out to our family friends as clients. My parents' friends wanted to be supportive, so they took a chance on me, which, unfortunately, did not always work out for them. The owner of the company, William Hamilton, was a very smart man and I was learning a lot from him. Sadly, though, one day when he did not show up for work, we learned that his small Cessna plane had crashed and he was dead. The company folded.

Next, I found work at a rent-to-own appliance company. A few months into my job, the company flew me to San Francisco for a paid business trip. This was my first time traveling for business. I had a free plane ticket and a paid-for hotel, and I was in San Francisco! Naturally, I stopped by Saks Fifth Avenue on the way from the airport to the hotel and treated myself to some retail therapy. When I got to the hotel, I realized I was late for the big meeting which was the reason for the trip. My boss called me to his room, berated me for being late, and told me I'd be fired if it happened again.

"Do you like this job?" he asked in his clipped middle manager voice as he slowly lowered himself onto the edge of the bed.

"Yeah, I do," I said. "I'm really sorry I was late," I stammered and looked down at my feet.

"Well," he said slowly, "if that's true, here's something you can do to make it up to me," he said as he unzipped his pants. This was my introduction to the "me too" movement, years before the phrase was coined. I didn't know I could say no. I'm from a generation where being sexually abused in the workplace was the norm, not the exception.

* * * * *

My next job would change the course of my life forever. In May 1974, I climbed the narrow staircase of an old, nondescript office building in downtown Las Vegas, which housed the Western Pacific Silver and Gold Exchange. I met and was interviewed by the CEO, who hired me on the spot.

I was proud of my new job title, Office Manager. I was in charge of customer relations. Western Pacific Silver and Gold Exchange was a newly formed company that sold silver bars, gold bullion, and coins. They promoted 30-, 60-, and 90-day delivery and provided a discount for buyers who bought now and took delivery later. The office comprised the entire second floor of the office building near Fremont Street in downtown Las Vegas.

Fremont Street was the original downtown business district where the Las Vegas Strip started. I can still remember driving down the famous street, seeing Trader Vic, the larger-than-life mechanical cowboy next to the Golden Nugget Casino, his cigarette dangling from his mouth and the smoke rising, and his automated arm moving back and forth as he loudly boomed "Howdy Partner," over and over again.

My high school friends and I used to go into the Horseshoe Casino on the weekends and get our picture taken in front of the million dollars in cash that was enticingly stacked and visible behind the thick plexiglass. Their blackjack tables had a single deck, which gave better odds. This was our Disneyland.

It was surreal to be working at this sophisticated company. The men wore suits and everyone projected an image of success and affluence. Being among this polished group of people made me feel important. I was happy to be there and wanted to be just like them. The leading members of the sales team, Becky and Allen, were a very good-looking married couple who had moved to Las Vegas from Atlanta. They were upbeat and always laughing. Everyone played golf together on the weekends.

When we met our sales goals, we were treated to lavish dinners out at restaurants on the strip, like The Sultan's Table in Caesars Palace and the Dome of the Sea in the Dunes Hotel. The Cristal champagne flowed while we women listened to the men strategize about the future of the company. This was a very fun job and I felt close to these people. They introduced me to self-improvement, goal setting, and manifesting what I wanted in life. This was my first introduction to Napoleon Hill's *The Laws of Success*, James Allen's *As a Man Thinketh*, and Og Mandino's *The Greatest Salesman in the World*. All of the employees were given these books and told to read and study them. These concepts were new to me and very compelling. I've now been following these principles for over 40 years, and I know they work.

The story of James Ray Houston was a big one in Las Vegas at the time. He was the owner of the company, a gregarious man with a large presence. The newspapers dubbed him the Silver King. James Ray was ambitious, and he was politically inclined. One day he called a meeting and told us that he had decided to run for governor. He saw the direction the city was going and wanted to make a difference. He was going to run as an Independent. We were surprised, but quickly got on board and supported him. He was a powerful force. In his book,

Countdown to Depression, he described how silver was the way to stay solvent. He was trying to wake people up about how the government was trying to control them and the economy by devaluing the dollar. His popularity was growing and the powers that be were not happy.

Las Vegas was a very small town and his flamboyant personality was making waves with the political powers that be. He did not know how to lay low or operate under the radar. He was getting a lot of attention. The company was on track and growing fast until a former security guard and disgruntled employee made allegations that the company was a scam and the vault was empty. This was a disaster for our boss's campaign for governor. We were constantly trying to put out fires. Things were heating up by the minute.

My new boss, Evan, ran the company. Evan was a Minnesota Viking type, with piercing blue eyes and an intensity about him that could not be missed. With a sharp intelligence, he was a military man who had narrowly escaped death in the Cuban missile crisis.

A few weeks after I started working for Evan, I started to develop feelings for him. He was 36 years old and I was 19. The age gap did not seem to make much difference— the problem was that he was married. His wife and three children lived in Minnesota while he was in Las Vegas trying to make his mark.

Over time, Evan and I built a strong connection, but I knew our affair needed to end. He was committed to his family, and I think the fact that he was not emotionally available struck a perfect, but unfortunate, chord in me— the chord I'd been playing my whole life that said I always had to "try harder." So, try harder, I did. I was the perfect worker by day and the perfect lover by night. But still, he left. He had to go home to his wife and kids.

I was hurt when Evan left Las Vegas. There was always a longing in me for the men I could not have. It replicated the feeling of the "daddy that got away," the one who had chosen to be with someone else.

Evan was my first mentor and he continued to correspond with me after I left the company, always building me up and telling me that I was exceptional and intelligent, not just beautiful.

I can still picture lying in bed with him in his high-rise condo at the Country Club Towers, looking out at the lights of the strip in Las Vegas. I felt safe and loved being with him, but I wanted more. His love and support helped to relieve the pain I felt over losing my parents. He was an anchor for me at the time. He knew me, he knew my friends, and he encouraged me to be my best self. He never did anything to intentionally hurt me. He cared about me. Looking back, I can see that I was attracted to smart men that I could not have—someone else already had them. Maybe that is what made them more attractive.

* * * * *

The Las Vegas Sun newspaper was covering the campaign's progress and our company was getting a lot of coverage.

The chain had quickly grown to eight locations in five cities with two off-site smelters. But James Ray's campaign for governor was ramping up and needed more and more money. The political powers that be were worried he was going to win.

One afternoon, a reporter from the local paper, *The Las Vegas Sun*, came to the counter posing as a customer and asking about our gold and silver businesses. We were all out of the office in an offsite meeting and the reporter bribed Rodney Franklin, a security guard, to let him see the vault. Because we offered 30-, 60-, and 90-day deliveries, we kept little stock on hand. There was an off-site smelter where the gold and silver bars were made before being shipped to the customers. Therefore, we did not keep all of the gold and silver bullion in the vault. But that didn't matter to this member of the press. This reporter took a picture of the empty vault, and he ran an article in the newspaper that was headlined

NO SILVER IN THE VAULT. This was the beginning of the smear campaign against James Ray and the first of many scare tactics imposed by the press.

The press started hounding James Ray and continued to smear him with damaging articles. Eventually, he left town, leaving all of us holding the bag. The company folded. Evan would take the fall and go to jail for mail fraud—the SEC said it was illegal to advertise that these silver and gold coins would increase in value. Becky and Allen left to sell timeshares in Florida, and James Ray's wife, Casey, and I, who had become friends, were left to our own devices.

James Ray Houston continued to be the topic of conversation. He was on the lam and, just like his counterpart, DB Cooper, was not found. He had a magnetic personality that drew people in. He had created a following and people had responded to his backstory of being a poor kid raised in the foster system who pulled himself up by selling mail-order puzzles. For a prize, people would send $8 cash in envelopes for the chance of winning the jackpot or sweepstakes. This is how he originally made his money. Small envelopes with cash would pour into the office daily. James Ray would be found and arrested two years later in Tampa, Florida, selling door-to-door vacuum cleaners. How quickly the mighty can fall.

The company was defunct and once again I was out of work. It was the end of an era.

* * * * *

Casey Houston was a petite blond woman who looked like she'd stepped out of a Chanel ad. We hit it off right away when I started working for her husband's company, and have now been friends for over 40 years. Casey and

James Ray lived in a 10,000-square-foot home in a ritzy area of Las Vegas, that *The Las Vegas Sun* called "The Palatial Palace." The rent was way too high for Casey to afford on her own, so she asked me to move in. She needed help with the bills and with her two small children from a prior marriage. So, I became Aunt Duffy! We were a family.

* * * * *

Casey, my new roommate, was older than me. She'd been around the block and was beautiful, smart, and savvy. Her husband's company was now defunct, his election for governor lost, and he was on the lam. I was out of a job and she had lost her main source of income. We were in a situation!

Then, she took me by the hand and said, "No one is coming to help us—we have to be able to support ourselves."

My mother had always modeled a great work ethic. She was a legal secretary and had helped me get summer jobs as a courthouse runner in her law firm when I was in high school, so I thought I might use that experience to get hired at a law firm.

With determination, I picked up the small Las Vegas Directory of Attorneys booklet that had been next to our phone at home and I began to call each law office and ask if they needed any help. One of the attorneys told me to come by for an interview. He ran a single-office family law practice. He helped people with their divorces, name changes, and adoptions.

Peter Costas sat behind his big mahogany desk, leaned back, chewing on a fat, smelly, unlit cigar, and looked at me intently with his piercing brown eyes.

"Okay," he said as I finished giving my work history. "You're hired."

It was my lucky break. He hired me and personally trained me. I was excited! After working in his office for six months, I did my first self-directed pleading—I typed and filed my own papers, changing my name from my stepfather's to my original last name given to me on my birth certificate. It was very satisfying. His name had never felt right to me. I was now no longer tied to my stepfather in any way. I had a good job, a new white Pontiac Trans Am, a great place to live, and life was going well. Until it wasn't.

Although I was making a decent living at the family law practice, money was still tight for Casey and me. But we were young and beautiful and decided to use what the good lord gave us.

We did our best to keep things afloat in the pink palatial palace, but eventually, it became too much with the press and the cops following us everywhere we went, asking about her husband. We decided to move. We needed to get to a place we could afford and where we could keep a lower profile. One day she introduced me to my first customer/barter arrangement. Today they call it sex work.

My first client's name was Leonard, and he owned a very popular apartment building in town called The Villas. It was more rent than we could afford but Casey made a deal with him to trade "rent" for "fun." It worked for him. Casey and I would trade off each month. He would arrive on the first of the month with a bottle of wine and collect the "rent."

Not having to pay the full rent helped, but it was not enough. I needed a side hustle.

I applied for a bookkeeping position at a local business called The Velvet Touch, a small business with a few massage parlors around town. I did my best, but numbers were not my strong suit and I was quickly in over my head. Luckily, though, the owner had gotten to know me and had other plans for me. He came to me with a new proposition—he had decided to expand his business by making "house calls."

As I climbed the stairs of the seedy motel in my high heels from Suzie Creamcheese, a trendy shoe store on the strip, I felt like a girl on the first day of school. Excited but nervous. Full of expectation. Dressed in my favorite white corduroy pantsuit, the one I'd made in home economics class with wide black velvet lapels adorned with red cherries. I felt so pretty. I loved this pantsuit. My grandmother was a seamstress and I knew that she'd be proud of me. I had inherited her sewing skills. A tall, bald, black man climbed the stairs ahead of me carrying a projector. We got to the top landing, found the right door, and I knocked.

"Velvet Touch," I said, and the door opened.

A shirtless, black man opened the door and looked me up and down, smiling. "Come in," he said, widening the door.

We walked in and my bodyguard began setting up the projector. The man was on the bed watching. He was old, had gray stubble, and looked dirty. Apprehension rose up in my gut.

What am I doing here? I thought to myself.

The bodyguard finished the setup of the video and said to the client, "That will be $200. Our girl here will show you the flick and you can do whatever comes naturally, but no touching her. She's just here to show the film."

The man grunted and handed him two crumpled-up bills. My guy shoved the money in his pocket, looked at me, and said, "I will be right outside. Have fun."

The door opened and closed, and he was gone. *I can't believe I'm doing this*, I thought to myself. The room was dark. I fumbled for the switch and turned on the projector and a black and white pattern flashed on the wall. An image of two girls and a guy came into view. One girl was kissing the guy on a couch and the other was unbuckling his pants.

The old guy on the bed said, "Hey, let's party."

"I'm just here to show the film," I said, very intent on manning the projector.

"Yeah, right," he grumbled. "I paid for a blow job."

"No," I stammered. "I don't do that." Suddenly, I

panicked, wondering how I was going to get out of there. I was scared. Just then the film busted and the white wall glared where there used to be porn. The sound kept playing so the noise of moans still filled the room.

I began to fiddle with the projector and nervously mumbled, "I'll have this fixed again in a bit."

But the film just kept flipping round and round on the wheel.

The man complained, "Hey, let's get this party started. I want what I paid for."

No no no no I can't do this. I can't I can't I can't...he's gross and I have to get out of here!

"I'll be right back," I said. I opened the door and ran outside where my guy was, at the bottom of the stairs, smoking. I blurted out, "I can't do it—the film broke and I have to go."

He looked at me and quickly threw the cigarette down.

"Get in the car," he said, handing me the keys.

He ran upstairs and packed up the equipment. Before long he was back, and we were driving.

"I had to give the money back," he said. "Not cool. Howard is not going to be happy." As we drove off, I sat looking out the car window wondering how my life had come to this. I tried to justify my behavior. I didn't ask for the money. I was just going to show a film, wasn't I? I was just trying to take care of myself. No one else was taking care of me. What was I supposed to do? I was on my own. No one cared. No one loved me.

These times were really hard for me. I truly felt alone. My stepfather, Ron, had moved on to his new life. My mother had remarried and left town. I was left to figure it out. Casey was my new anchor. With her husband a fugitive, she and I were capsized in the ocean, clinging to this life raft. We needed to save ourselves.

We were young and beautiful and alone. We needed more money. We began to dabble in the escort service, accompanying high rollers. They came to Las Vegas ready to party and they didn't want to do it alone. They wanted a pretty girl on their arm to drink, dine, and gamble with. Did they want more than that? Of course. But for the right price, we were willing. We only needed to find a few regulars to supplement our income and things would be good. For me, there was a lumber magnate who loved to take me to a live show and then back to his room. There was the St. Louis attorney who wrote me poetry on cocktail napkins. The Mexican cartel boss, Fernando, who stole my heart. I justified it all by telling myself that it was no different from normal dating. On a traditional date, I would meet a guy, hang out, go to dinner, and have sex. This was the same, only more fun and more lucrative. The guy would take me to a fancy dinner or show and then we would gamble, and he would share his winnings with me and then we'd have sex. Same thing as a normal date— only better. Like Sharon Stone in the Scorsese movie, *Casino*, I was a survivor and needed to make things happen. I feel that movie was written for me. I was working it to the best of my ability, and I was on a roll.

But the other shoe was about to drop.

I got a call that I should have realized right away was not right.

"I got your number from Casey," the voice on the phone said.

"I'm only here for a couple of days, but I'm wondering if you'd like to meet."

"Sure," I said. "Let's do it."

"Great," the voice said. "I'm at the Sahara. I'll meet you in the sports bar in an hour."

I thought this was a client that Casey had connected with, so I didn't hesitate to meet him. I pulled into the vestibule of the Sahara Hotel in my white TransAm with the tee tops removed and handed the bellman a $20.

"Keep it up front please, I won't be long."

"Sure," he said, smiling, taking the bill, and sliding expertly into the car. It was a hot day and I had on white shorts, a crop top, four-inch cork espadrilles, and a wide-brimmed hat. The huge glass doors opened automatically, and the coolness of the inside casino welcomed me like a long-lost friend. I found a seat in the sports bar and was soon approached by a tall, tan, good-looking guy with dark hair. As he walked up to me, he removed his Ray-Ban glasses. I smiled. He smiled. We were making random chit-chat when a cocktail waitress walked up to us and offered him two room keys she had on a tray.

"Thanks," he nodded at her, picking up the keys as she

quickly retreated. "Do you want to go to my room?" he asked.

"Okay," I replied.

If I had not been so young and naive, I would have known how unlikely that was and would have recognized it as a setup. But I had never even rented a hotel room before and did not know how it worked.

"Wait ten minutes and then come up," he said.

"Okay," I said.

I took the key he handed me and after 10 minutes went to his room. The door was slightly open and I entered the room, looking around at the neat queen-sized bed and the dresser with the TV on it.

"I'm here," I said nervously, getting my bearings.

"Get undressed," he called out to me from the bathroom. "I'll be right out."

I removed my clothes and quickly got under the sheets. He came out with just his boxers on, put a $100 bill on the dresser, and climbed into bed next to me.

"Hello," he said and began kissing me.

Just as I was beginning to relax, I felt him pull away, sit up, and say,

"Vice... Debbie, you're under arrest,"

As he held up his Las Vegas Metro Police badge, I could feel the blood quickly drain from my body. I was so scared, I could not move.

This must be a dream! I thought to myself. I was the daughter of a cop and this is not how I was raised.

Suddenly, the door opened, and two more men dressed in suits burst into the room.

"Stand up," one of the detectives said. He pulled me from the bed and made me stand there, naked, in front of them. The guy that set me up grabbed a towel from the bathroom and handed it to me. I clutched the towel and was frantically trying to cover myself, when one of the other guys began taking pictures of me. They told me to turn front, sideways, and back. I was mortified.

"Tell me where James Ray Houston is," the short one said.

"I don't know," I said.

"We know you know, and if you don't tell us, you're going to jail," he continued.

"We've been following you," said Agent X, the guy who'd set me up. "We want to know where James Ray is."

"I don't know where he is!" I cried.

"Well, you live with his wife, so I suggest you find out," he shot back. "And then you call me. We aren't going to arrest you today." He flipped his business card onto the dresser and said, "I'll be in touch."

They left, leaving me alone in the room, shaking and crying. I did not know what to do. I was a 19-year-old girl, trying to fend for herself in a place I should not be. I felt helpless and alone. For a long time, I could not move. Eventually, I got dressed and returned home in a daze.

Weeks later, I was at work when my stepfather, Ron, called. "Can you come meet me for lunch?" he asked.

"Okay," I said, and agreed to come to his office. His office was the police station. When I got there, a uniformed officer led me to a room where Ron was seated behind a small metal desk. This was an interrogation room. My palms were sweaty.

"Hi," I said.

"Hi," he returned evenly.

We looked at each other for a moment, and then he opened the drawer in front of him and threw three Polaroid pictures onto the gray Formica surface between us. "What would YOU say if your boss called you into his office and told you that your daughter was a hooker?" he demanded.

I looked at him stunned. I did not know what to say. I glanced at the black and white picture of the frightened girl clutching the towel to her body and said nothing.

"They are looking for James Ray Houston. Do you know where he is?" Ron asked.

"No," I said truthfully.

"This would kill your mother, you know," he said.

But my mother has left me, the thoughts resonated in my head. *She married a man she'd only known for three weeks and she left town. Left me on my own—for Utah.* Both Ron and I were grieving and dealing with the loss in our own way, and this incident did not help.

I returned to work that afternoon, trying to act as though nothing had happened. I tried to focus on the work at hand, but I was distracted, and my boss, the attorney, noticed.

"What's up with you today?" he asked.

After I'd returned the same pleading to him three times with multiple errors, he asked again, "You okay?"

This time I sat down with a long sigh. After a few stops and starts I told him the whole story and began to cry as I let out all the details of what I'd gone through in the last few months. He looked at me, put down his cigar, and came around the desk to where I was seated. He drew me to him in a fatherly hug and told me that everything would be okay.

Shortly after, he left the office, and when he returned, he said to me, "The matter is closed. Your file has been sealed and no one will ever bring it up again."

I could not believe my ears. This man was my hero. I was so relieved. Someone had finally stepped up for me.

I was mortified at what had happened, especially since my stepfather was a detective and his boss had shown him the pictures. I was so grateful to my boss for covering it up. He was a family man 30 years older than me with three kids. I really trusted him and was shocked when, not long after, he said he wanted to see what the other guys got to see. In other words, quid pro quo. Of course. This was Las Vegas. He would make a point to drop by my apartment every couple of weeks with his smelly chewed cigar, and the guy I had thought walked on water was just another guy who wanted his pound of flesh.

I needed to put this behind me and move on. It was time to leave the one-man office and take on more responsibility.

* * * * *

After perusing the want ads for several weeks, I saw that the Dunes Hotel & Country Club, a casino on the Las Vegas strip, was hiring someone to work in the executive office. They wanted someone with a legal background and I knew I fit the bill perfectly. I applied for the job and was hired. I would be working for the owner and CEO in the executive office. This was going to change my life. I gave notice at the family law office and never looked back.

Although I was raised in Las Vegas, I'd rarely been to the strip. This was a very new experience for me. The town was run by people who had come here looking for a piece of the action and misfits who could escape their past, blend in, reinvent themselves, and be a part of a new growth opportunity. Given my experience, I know that I am lucky to be alive. Many of my friends were not so lucky.

Sin City, as it was affectionately called, was a small, unregulated town, and it was growing fast. It was a western town with businesses that operated 24-hours, seven-days-a-week, and the grocery stores had slot machines. Organized crime saw an opportunity and began to move in.

Las Vegas looked glamorous from the outside, but inside was anything but. When I was young, my dad worked all night, came home in the morning, and slept all day.

I thought these things were normal. I didn't know the difference. The rules didn't apply to our family. Ron could do whatever he wanted. Drive fast, chase a fire with a gun in the car, target practice in the desert. If my mom or I got stopped for speeding, we simply smiled and said,

"Oh, do you know my father, Ron Olthoff? He's with Metro."

They would immediately wave us on with a smile and a "slow down!"

Raised in a conservative family, I had rarely been to the strip before age 18. I was a brownie, a Girl Scout, a rainbow girl, and had a confirmation in the Lutheran church at 16. This was all new. The casinos, the celebrities, the showgirls, the lights. It was a lot to take in.

Gradually, I learned that Las Vegas was a "you scratch my back, I'll scratch yours" kind of town. Everyone had their hand out and everything could be accomplished if you knew the right people.

My new boss was a St. Louis attorney infamous for representing Jimmy Hoffa, who, at the time, had been missing for a while. Mr. S was scary. He was larger than life. He had a heavy Yiddish accent and was very intimidating. I found my way into his heart by organizing his world. It was my superpower to go through all of the papers on his messy desk and when he'd say, "Where is this or that," I would know. I would direct him right to it.

"Here you go, boss," I would say. I impressed him, and he liked me. It also might have been my youthful bubbly personality, my size 36DD breasts, or my bouncy blond curls, but I like to think that he saw something in me.

This was a fun job and it came with certain perks. They started me at the front desk and I was handling the phones for three of the top executives of the hotel at that time.

"Executive office," I said clearly and authoritatively when a call came in.

"Hello, darling, is he in?" a well-modulated British accent asked.

"May I tell him who's calling?" I asked professionally.

"It's Cary," the man replied.

OMG! Cary Grant, I squealed to myself but remained cool. It was my first day and I was the receptionist. This involved taking the calls for Mr. S. I was in charge of his large, red leather-bound book. I would list every call that came into the executive office and when he came in, I would take the book to him for review. He would put a large circle by the names of the people he wanted to speak to. I would then get them on the line and transfer the call to him. The names were of powerful people, politicians, and movie stars like Don Rickles, Charlie Rich, Cary Grant, Al Dorfman, Bernie Sindler, and Myron Lansky.

These were exciting and very interesting times. I'd been working at The Dunes for about a year when a culinary strike shut down the bar and the restaurants because the union employees were not allowed to enter the hotel. To keep the revenue flowing into the hotel, executives began to let the non-union employees do other jobs. So even though I was not yet 21, I got to serve drinks in the bar downstairs. It was a very intense and unusual time and the employees bonded over it.

I was the youngest secretary that had ever worked in the executive office, and the day I turned 21, Charlie Rich, one of the owners of the hotel, gave me 21 rolls of dimes so that I could play the slot machines. *Disneyland, indeed.*

* * * * *

Working in the executive office gave me power. The pit bosses were friendly to me. I could get dinners comped for my friends and family at the five-star restaurant in the hotel.

It was my 21st birthday, and after treating my mom and a few friends to a delicious dinner at the hotel's Dome of the Sea, we passed by the hotel jeweler who was standing in front of his shop near the casino.

"How's it going, Deborah?" he asked as I walked by.

"Great!" I said. "It's my birthday."

"Really?" he said. "Happy Birthday!" and with that he opened the large black velvet case he was holding. "Pick one," he said, smiling. I stood there mesmerized, looking at all of the beautiful rings shining up at me from their black velvet case.

"Anything you want, honey," he said.

My eyes fell on a beautiful gold and diamond cluster. I tried it on.

"It's gorgeous," I said, eyes glowing.

"It's yours," he said. "A beautiful ring for the beautiful lady."

I was so incredibly touched. For years that ring was a touchstone of memories for a young girl coming into her own. What a nice gesture, you might be thinking. What a kind man. Not really. He knew that I was the CEO's secretary and if he needed anything, he now had someone in the executive office that was on his side. He was hedging his bets for the future.

* * * * *

One morning, while reviewing the Room, Food, and Beverage ("RFB") reports at work, I saw a name that I recognized. I was going over the daily roster that showed which known high rollers were staying at the hotel, and those who were cleared for free RFB privileges when I recognized the name Robert Bernard, a man my mother had dated briefly. I called him up and made a plan to go to dinner with him. My mom was married by now and living out of town with her new husband, so, *why not*, I rationalized. After dinner, we went back to his room and had sex. *What was I thinking?* WAS I thinking? I knew full well this had been my mother's boyfriend, and I pursued him. Was this a direct fuck you to her? Why? Because she had abandoned me. She'd married someone she'd known for three weeks and left town with him. I was pissed. I was young. Unequipped to deal with my feelings. I remember thinking, *Mom, this is what you should have done. We would have been in a much better financial situation if you'd let Bob get close to you.* He had wanted her to move to Miami, but she was too afraid to pursue it. I resented her for not being able to find a man or father figure who would provide a stable and secure environment for us. Looking back now, I can see the unhealthy competition that was at work between us. I did not know where she ended and where I began. I was hungry for attention and love, and this was my way of getting it.

This event caused me so much shame over the years. Although the behavior was unconscious on my part, I was so ashamed that I'd let it happen. Looking back now, I can see that my promiscuity was a direct result of the trauma I experienced in my early years. I had no feelings for this man. He was a virtual stranger, yet, at that moment, he connected me to my mother.

I felt devastated learning that my father was not my real dad, and I felt abandoned by my mother. I was left. I was hurt and angry. For years, anger was one of the only emotions I recognized when asked how I felt and it was the driving force behind all of the choices in my life. My unresolved trauma was at the root of all of my psychological misdeeds.

* * * * *

Two of the young casino executives were my boss's son and nephew. While not my direct bosses, they felt they had power over me and they wanted to wield it. They were pit bosses and controlled the casino and the players. They also felt they controlled me. They began to pressure me to date the players. These were high rollers who came in from

Miami on the junkets. One of these players was Fernando. We had dinner when he was in town and he took me to Mexico City and Acapulco. He was tall, rich, young, and handsome. I was smitten. He was married.

This was getting out of hand and not what I signed up for. The people at the job I loved were beginning to use me.

It was not a surprise, since I have a long history of being abused by men. Beginning with the early trauma of losing my biological father as a baby, enduring physical abuse from my stepfather Ron, being raped at 15, and then having my world fall apart at 16 when I discovered my dad was not my real father.

This was a seedy time. I was of legal age and completely out of control.

My all-time low was the doctor who dispensed drugs in exchange for sex.

My friends and I were sitting in the waiting room, comparing notes on last night's date, when a sour-faced nurse came in and barked in a clipped tone, "The doctor will see you now."

We got up and followed her to the exam room where she opened the door and we entered, squeezing past her. The doctor was at the small sink washing his hands, his back to us.

"What do you girls need today?" he asked with a smile.

We were there to get diet pills and Quaaludes, the popular drugs at the time. Dr. P was a short, fat, jovial, Mormon man who had girls lining up to get what he was passing out. We put in our order and he hastily scribbled something on a pad of paper, tore off the sheet, and set it down.

He then plopped his full girth down into the brown Naugahyde chair in the corner, patted his lap, and said, "Come here pretty girl, and have a seat." As if we were taking castor oil, we dutifully obliged and gave him head to get the pills we wanted. This new skill I had acquired proved to be as valuable as the shorthand I'd learned in high school. His eventual arrest came as no surprise to anyone. The seven-count indictment charged Dr. P with "illegal distribution of various controlled substances," which were responsible for so many overdoses of the patients he prescribed to.

* * * * *

Las Vegas was going through growing pains over the clash between the corrupt politicians and the mafia-controlled casinos. It was a wild time. The mob had moved in and there were a lot of power struggles. Disputes were settled with fists and force. Drugs were rampant and people were ending up in the desert, buried alive or dumped in bags. I needed to break free. My boss's niece, Nadia, was the house counsel, and she and I had become friends. When she invited me to move to Los Angeles with her and share an apartment, I jumped at the chance. I was taking the geographical cure.

CHAPTER 5

Love Junkie

It was March of 1977 when I moved to Los Angeles looking for a fresh start and excitement. And I found it.

Driving up the Pacific Coast Highway in my 450 SL, top down, blond hair flying, and Journey's "Faithfully" blasting through my Bose speakers, smelling the salt air, and watching the waves crash on the rocks was like a dream come true. I was so happy to be away from the harsh, hot desert of Las Vegas. I loved living near the ocean and seeing it every day. I felt so alive and full of anticipation and hope. My job was going well and I hoped it would blossom into a career. I had a semi-safety blanket in that I was employed by Leonard, my boyfriend at the time. He was married, but he and his wife lived in another state so he was not too concerned. Neither was I. He came to LA twice a week on business and it worked for us both.

This man shaped a big part of my life. He hired me away from the Dunes Hotel in Las Vegas to move to LA and run his real estate development company. Things had become complicated at the Dunes and this was perfect timing. This was to be my new beginning.

I got my real estate license. I ran his company. I sold condos. Together, we'd built this building from the ground up. It was a 20-story high-rise in Westwood along the Wilshire corridor. I learned a lot from Leonard. He was a shrewd businessman and a very tough negotiator. He never gave anything away for free and he never left money on the table. He taught me so much about business. When I arrived, I was an ambitious girl from a small town, set free in the big city, Los Angeles, the City of Angels. Combustible.

Leonard would fly into town in the morning. We would work until lunch. Have sex. Go back to work. Go out to dinner. Have sex. Do it again the next day.

Besides growing my business acumen, another thing I loved about our arrangement was that I was getting to see the best of LA, Hollywood, and Beverly Hills. Each week, we would go to a new restaurant that I chose and I was crossing them off a list in a book I had, *Los Angeles' Best Restaurants*. I loved LaScala, Perrino's, The Bistro Gardens, and later meeting with Wolfgang Puck when he ran his original pizza restaurant, Spago. After we'd completed the five-star route, we started on the trendy. We loved the Mustache Café, Bicycle Club, Musso & Franks, and The Alley. Honestly, I loved restaurants, and I loved that when I was with him, it was *carte blanche*. We'd start with appetizers and end with desserts with wine and drinks to accompany it. Dinners were more of the same, and in the evening, we included nightclubs.

Leonard had a lot of energy, which was a plus because I got to see the best discos and clubs that LA had to offer. One night, we double-dated with Leonard's friend, Frank, the owner of a chain of lumber stores. After the four of us had eaten a delicious dinner at Nick's Seafood, we crossed Sunset Boulevard where it met Crescent Heights, and walked into a tall office building. Frank walked over to the guard on duty, leaned into him as he pressed a folded-up bill into his hand, and spoke something into his ear. The guard nodded, opened the elevator door, and invited us in.

Once inside, he turned a private key, and the elevator took us down to a floor below the basement. The door opened to reveal a club blasting Motown music with a sea of people gyrating rhythmically to the beat. As we walked in, we could see that, although we were the only white people there, we were basically unnoticed by the patrons, who were all engaged in a rousing New York hustle to a popular Earth, Wind & Fire song. This was a magical night and I felt transported to another world. It was so new and exciting.

When the bar closed at 2 am, the four of us walked outside and Frank handed me the keys to his Rolls Royce and said,

"You drive, babe, you're the most sober."

We climbed into the beautiful classic Rolls with the gold-winged angel on the hood and headed back to the Marina.

"G'night y'all, come back again," the valet yelled after us.

There was no chemistry with Leonard, but I loved his mind. He did not bring out the intensity in me. Even though he was a private person, unavailable to most, he was available to me. I could always reach him, and I knew that he loved me. But there was no heat. It was a business transaction and it suited us both. I loved being exposed to the glamor and sophistication of the restaurants.

* * * * *

One day, I met Henry, who was Leonard's architect at Condo West, the real estate development company where I worked. He was hired to work on an apartment/condo conversion project and I was the construction manager. He was talented and had so much passion, which was evident as I watched him draft his architectural drawings and describe the plans that he had for the units.

Even though he was 40 years old, I was attracted to him. Looking back now, I'm wondering why, at 22, I was involved with a man so much older. With Leonard, it was because there was a monetary payoff involved. But not so with Henry. I just thought Henry was sexy and sweet. He had salt and pepper gray hair and a beard and drove a classic red Corvette. He was also smart and funny with an adorable Irish brogue. His accent reminded me of my Irish heritage and the father I'd never known. After work, we would drive to the local Molly Malone bar, drink shots and play darts. He adored me and I suppose I was always drawn to men who appeared to be smarter and more accomplished than me, who showered me with adoration. I was looking for the Good Daddy. Unfortunately, as it turned out, Henry was anything but.

Henry was a high-functioning alcoholic by day, competent and creative, but after work, he needed to decompress and his demons would come out. Being an alcoholic, he was the broken bird I wanted to fix. Seeing the situation now, I was more his babysitter than his girlfriend. I would stay with him in his little apartment, watching TV and having sex with him as he drank his sherry and smoked his cigarettes until he fell asleep— usually in an upright position. Then, I would slip out from under his arm and escape to the fresh air and freedom. He was very possessive of me and would call me when he came to and angrily ask, "Where'd ya go babe, why did you leave?"

Oh, I dunno, I thought to myself, *I finished cleaning your apartment and I got lonely and bored and decided to rejoin my own world.*

He was an empty well—I got nothing from him. There were no dates, no dinners, or flowers. One day after I'd broken up with him, he called me at work and threatened to kill me. I laughed it off and hung up on him, returning my attention to the prospective buyers in front of me. Soon after, in the lobby of the condominium building where I worked, my attention was on the plans spread out in front of me. Suddenly I heard a loud commotion, looked up and saw a rabid man charging toward me. Henry, his face contorted and yelling something I couldn't understand, lunged over the desk, his hands finding my neck and knocking me down with his full weight. Thankfully, someone called 911 and he was taken away in handcuffs. I seemed to have a knack for pissing men off.

Since leaving home in Las Vegas, and now living on my own in Los Angeles, there was a cornucopia of men to draw from working at this construction site and condominium project. I was the girlfriend of the owner, but I entertained myself on the side. There was Chip, an amazing-looking, tall, fit construction worker. He was just a bit of fun, but we did enjoy each other's company.

Then, there was Norm, Chip's boss, who owned the construction company. He was going through a divorce and was also fun for a time. There was Mark, the fabulously good-looking pharmacy student from USC. He seemed to have no vices. He was somewhat boring to me—I guess I needed them to be a little messed up. But he was great to look at and very smart. We had good chemistry. He was a college student, so he had no money. That didn't really fit my picture, so the affair was short-lived.

It was now six months after I'd arrived in town. I was 23 years old, had a new job with a promising future, drove a beautiful gold Mercedes Benz 450 SL, and lived in the Marina. Marina del Rey. Life was good.

One summer day, returning home from the market, I pulled up to the stoplight and looked over at the sleek black Cadillac convertible with a gorgeous man with olive skin and wild, curly, black hair looking over and smiling at me. He had a darling little boy with him with huge brown eyes and the same curly hair. He was peeking around his dad's shoulder and smiling at me too. These two were irresistible. Each of us, convertible tops down, music blasting, stopped at the signal only a few feet away.

"Can we make it?" the man yelled over at me.

"Can we make it?" *Make what?* I thought. This was weird.

"Make what?" I yelled back.

"Dinner tonight!"

"Oh," I said, suddenly understanding, "Yes!" I said, smiling and nodding my head up and down.

"Great," he said as the light turned green. "What's your number?" he asked, not moving the car.

I quickly called the number out and sped away. The rest is history. History in that this man changed my life. Turned it upside down.

Here I was, in a new job and dating the boss. My worldly possessions, overhead expenses, and new Mercedes were all a by-product of my boss/boyfriend. Falling in love with a hot new guy was not in the plan. But, I had a two-day-per-week commitment with Mr. MARRIED BOSS. Being conservative or practical was not in my wheelhouse. I threw caution to the wind and it was on.

The man in the Cadillac, whose name I learned was Amir, was Persian. It was 1977, and he, like so many others, had fled his country to escape the revolution. He and his son, Bijan, came to California under the guise of being on vacation. He told his ex-wife in Iran that he wanted to take his son to Disneyland and he would be back in three weeks. Instead, he left everything behind and came to California with his son and a suitcase full of cash and never looked back. His father was a general in the Shah's army. He came from a good family. He was a CPA by trade in his home country, however, he couldn't practice here.

So, he bought a car wash and set out to make his fortune in America.

Amir was very passionate. He was ethnic—different. He was sexy. He was crazy about me and he needed me. I was alone in a new city and we became an instant family. We used to return home from our respective jobs and cook dinner together in his little apartment in Culver City. He was intent on teaching me Farsi.

"Bedaman," he would say. I would look at him quizzically. "Give it to me," he would say, handing me the cup in his hand. He would make me tea. Persian tea.

"Chai McKai?" (*Do you want tea?*) he would ask, handing me tea and reciting the word for tea in Farsi.

"Merci Azezam," (*Thank you, darling*), I would respond, taking the tea from his hand. We would sit on the floor on large beautifully embroidered pillows, sip tea, and talk about our day.

"Boos kan," he said. "Kiss me!"

My Farsi vocabulary grew and grew and soon I was fluent and could join in the gatherings with his friends and understand most of what was going on.

One night after dinner, he pulled out a long, ornate ceramic pipe and put something in the hole at the end of it that looked like a piece of tootsie roll. He squished the soft, sticky, substance into the hole in the glass bulb and lit it. A sweet, rich, erotic smell wafted around me.

"Bokan," (*Take some*), he said, waving his hand around the smoke. I did. The feeling was unlike anything I'd ever experienced. It was opium and the high was unbelievable.

Looking back, I can see how I was willing to fly by the seat of my pants without any thought of what was good for me. I was young and I was reckless. I thought I was bulletproof.

I should have known something was wrong when I came out from his hole-in-the-wall apartment one morning to find my new Mercedes coupe riddled with dents from rocks and dirt. I was in the wrong place at the wrong time. Someone had obviously not appreciated me spending the night with him. But I ignored it and continued the relationship. I had found my latest project. I threw caution to the wind and buckled up for my latest wild ride.

Before long, my feelings for Amir had become so strong that I could not continue to see Leonard. We were in love. But this proved to be an expensive decision. Leonard, jealous and angry, informed me that I was fired and would have to return the car and the furniture that I'd been given by the company. It was difficult for me, but I knew that it was the right thing, and I agreed. I borrowed money from a friend and bought Leonard out of the car he'd purchased for me and made a payment arrangement for the furniture. Before long, I had a new job and I was ready to start my next chapter.

Since being fired by Leonard, I made less money and struggled to keep everything afloat on my own without being subsidized. I did not want to lose the condo that I'd purchased with his assistance.

Amir needed a green card and I needed help with the bills. He moved into my condo and agreed to pay the mortgage, and in return, I agreed to marry him.

We flew to Las Vegas for the quintessential shotgun wedding. I wore my Jordache jeans, a white lace top, and white satin high heels and he wore matching Jordache Jeans with a white gauzy shirt. It was pretty bohemian, actually. My mom arrived at the Las Vegas McCarran airport to pick us up in a beautiful cherry red Cadillac convertible, with her best friend Peggy in tow. They had agreed to be our witnesses. They drove us to the courthouse where we got our marriage license and then drove to the Little Chapel of the West where we proceeded to tie the knot. It was like a scene out of the Kardashians. My mother was crying, and Peggy was drunk off her ass. To this day I do not have a picture of this event. Sometimes I think maybe this impromptu wedding ceremony performed with a cubic zirconia ring never happened. But actually, I did marry him. I got my bills paid and he got his citizenship. There was no reception, honeymoon, or even a proper wedding dinner. We flew straight home and had a pre-packaged cheese sandwich on the plane.

It is pathetic how little you are willing to settle for, I mused to myself as I chewed the cold, gummy meal.

Our union lasted seven years. We went through a lot together. I became pregnant and he was excited, but I was apprehensive. I knew better than to have a child with this man. He was a workaholic, a volatile person, and a drug addict. I was not going to have his children. I was already raising the one he had. Instead, I scheduled an abortion. He was not happy. He was angry that I would do that, but I knew it was right for me. On the scheduled day, he dropped me at the clinic on his way to work and did not even take me in. My mother flew in to take me home after the surgery and tucked me into bed.

My husband and I went back to our routine of working all day and then coming home at night to the drug du jour after putting my stepson to bed. We would begin the all-night ritual of smoking freebase cocaine until four or five in the morning and then I would sleep two hours and drive to Century City to work all day at a very busy law office.

I loved this job and was grateful to have found it so quickly after being let go due to Leonard's jealousy.

I was underweight, stressed out, and undernourished. I was whacked out and drained from the lack of sleep, but still showed up to my job every day and tried to appear normal and competent. These episodes would go on for weeks on end and I knew this was not right. This was not the way I was raised. I was living a double life and became more and more distant from my friends and family. Amir was happy to keep me isolated. He had no interest in westernizing and liked to stay with his friends from back home where he could continue to speak Farsi and talk about the old days.

My friends did not know what was going on. I worked all day and came home to Amir and Bijan at night. We continued our crazy routine. The more drugs we did, the more addicted we became. I'm surprised that my brain functioned at all! I could see my husband's personality change for the worse and I knew that it was not right. He became more and more sexually depraved and tried to use his power as my drug supplier to get me to do things with other men and women. He would spend hours trying to talk me into bringing in another person. He would call people from sex lines and let them come to our home at all hours of the night. Chippendale's Male Dance Review was popular, and after the show, he would go get a dancer and bring them home and invite them to share in the drugs with us and then try to get me to have sex with them. I refused.

I began to hate him. The drugs were becoming more and more important to him. He was rarely sober. We would fight constantly. I was desperate to end this insanity. Naively, I would break the crack pipes and flush the coke down the toilet in the hopes of ending the madness that had become my life. To no avail; more drugs would always appear.

* * * * *

We'd been broken up for a few weeks when one day the phone rang.

"Azezam," he said, "I miss you."

"I miss you too," I said, hugging the phone to my ear. His deep voice was a salve to the open wound that used to be my heart.

"Beah," he said, (*Come now*) "Man McKhom" (*I want you*).

It was the middle of the afternoon and Bijan was in school until 5 pm. The longing took over and I could not get over this strong bond we had, so I agreed.

"I'm on my way," I said.

I walked into the small apartment with the Persian rugs hanging on the walls and the pillows on the floor instead of furniture. He threw a few pillows in the corner next to a low three-legged coffee table with a brass tray for a top and guided me to sit down. Once we were settled and after some small talk, avoiding the bigger issues, he pulled a tiny white envelope from his pocket, unfolded it, and shook some of the brown powder onto a piece of foil. He was close enough that I could smell the familiar intoxicating smell that drew me to him. He lit a match and ran the flame back and forth under the foil slowly until smoke began to rise up. As the drug began crackle and cook on the foil, he put it under my nose and instructed me to "breathe it in, breathe it in."

This was my introduction to heroin. It was called "chasing the dragon," and the physical reaction was fierce. Right away, I jumped up, ran to the bathroom, and threw up. But soon after, it was the most wonderful feeling. I felt that I was floating on clouds and it seemed like there was no one in the world but us two. Before long, my body was addicted and I needed this drug. He was my supplier. I did what he said so that I could get the drug. He had all the power now.

We reunited once again. One day in May, my mother was expected to visit to celebrate my birthday. We had stayed up all night long doing coke and heroin. It was 6 am and my mother was set to arrive in two and a half hours. I needed to pull it together, clean up the remnants of the night before, and get the house looking normal. My stepson would be waking up soon. I grabbed an open Diet Coke on the dresser and took a long swig. As I swallowed, I noticed something stuck to my tongue. I spit and peeled the small paper off and threw it in the trash, not thinking much of it at the time. Then, in the shower a short time later, a strange feeling washed over me. The hot water was cascading down, and I became mesmerized by the droplets falling all around me. The water seemed to be dancing in slow motion on the shower floor in technicolor. Something was terribly wrong.

I learned later that Amir had put a tab of acid in the Coke can and I was coming on to LSD. I don't know how long I was in there and the rest of the day was a blur but this is the type of person I was living with. I did my best to "maintain," and got through the day without my mother finding out what had happened (I think). I will never forget that incident.

That was a new low. Who would do that to someone? I could not come back from that experience. I knew that it was over between Amir and me but I decided to get him some help to cure his addiction. The irony is that I still wasn't thinking that *I* had a problem.

* * * * *

It was Thanksgiving and we had gone to Las Vegas to visit my mother and her husband, Richard. They had decided that Salt Lake City was not for them, and had moved back to Las Vegas. Amir had agreed to try to stay straight and had left his drugs at home. We were sightseeing at the Hoover Dam an hour away from my mom's house.

As the day wore on, Amir broke out in a sweat and began to cry that he needed to go to the hospital. We got him there as quickly as possible, but his condition was worsening by the moment. He was sweating and squirming and grimacing. We spent that night in the emergency room trying to get him some help, but they would not issue him any medication. We ended up just driving back to LA so that he could get his drugs. My family pretended that nothing was wrong. They looked the other way. This kind of thing did not happen in my family. My dad was a cop and my uncle was a judge, for God's sake.

After this event, Amir tried to make it up to me in an attempt to save our relationship, and we flew to Hawaii. However, each hour that went by in the plane, I saw him get more and more agitated and distressed. Sweat formed on his forehead and upper lip. His nose began to run. Five hours later, upon landing, he announced that he had to go back home. I could not believe what I was hearing. He boarded another flight on the spot and returned home and I spent a week alone in Hawaii. This was almost the end.

To support his growing habit and subsidize his business, Amir began to sell coke. He bought it, cut it, and cooked it. He sold rock cocaine. He spent long periods of time in the bathroom behind a locked door where he weighed, measured, and portioned the drugs into little paper packets to be sold. People began to come to my home at all hours.

I was trying to pretend that this was not happening. I was trying to put on a façade of normalcy for my stepson. In an attempt at family time, we would try to get Amir to take us to a movie on the weekend or out to dinner, but invariably he would not leave the house, and Bijan and I would go alone. I should have run from my husband and never looked back, but I could not. I called this sickness love. Another broken bird that I was going to fix.

Returning from the week alone in Hawaii, I broke up with him for the last time. This time I meant it. He packed up and left. One day, not long after, the phone rang.

"LA County Correctional calling with a collect call from Amir Pasha—do you accept?"

"Uh, yeah," I stammered.

"Debi Joun, you have to get me out."

"What did you do?" I asked.

"Uh, I sold some doo doo to a friend and she was a cop."

He had been arrested for selling drugs to an undercover police officer. I was devastated but instead of cutting off all ties, I jumped into fix-it mode.

Thus began the drama of me bailing him out, finding a lawyer (who was one of his clients—so a real loser already), and taking on the full-time care of Bijan. Amir got out on bail and started living on his own, but his behavior continued to escalate. He was on a tear, and it got worse.

I think back to that day:

One day, we had a plan that I would bring Bijan to visit Amir for the day. I'd been caring for Bijan full-time since Amir went to jail. Now that he was out, I continued to be his sole caregiver while Amir got on his feet. Bijan and I were doing our best to cope with our emotions and anxiety about the future. At the appointed time, we drove to Culver City and found the address of the apartment Amir had given me. We knocked on the door and were greeted by one of Amir's cronies that I'd met before. She ushered us into a dark, stale-smelling apartment and told us to "wait here."

Bijan and I sat on the couch alone for what seemed like a long time, waiting for Amir to come out. This was very familiar to me and reminded me of how I would wait for hours for Amir to come out of the bathroom at our home where he would be packaging his drugs to sell. I did not miss this.

"Are you hungry?" I asked Bijan, knowing it was close to lunchtime.

"Yeah..." he began. Suddenly, four men in black SWAT uniforms burst through the door and yelled,

"On the floor, NOW!"

Bijan and I were quickly thrown face down on the floor with shotguns to our heads and we saw Amir being dragged out of the bathroom and hauled outside. On his way out, as he moved past me, panic in his eyes, he said,

"Call Larry."

Larry Goldstein was his attorney. Bijan and I, completely shaken up, were questioned, and after proving that we had no involvement, were released and free to go. We headed to the station to bail out Amir and I felt so angry that I was once again pulled into this drama and craziness.

Amir's case eventually went to trial. Not surprisingly,

he lost the case and went to jail to serve a three-year sentence for drug trafficking. Then it was just Bijan and me. I felt helpless. Both of my drugs had been taken away—my dysfunctional love attachment and my coke/heroin/opium cocktail. I did not know what to do.

All I knew was that I needed to survive and take care of Bijan. I was working at the law office by day, and cooking and helping with homework by night. I was depressed and strung out. Soon after his incarceration, I got a call from one of Amir's friends who invited me to his house to get high. It was 2 am and he lived about 40 minutes away. I am ashamed to say that I left Bijan at home sleeping and I got in the car and drove to that guy's house and got high with him. Even as I dressed and went out into the cold, dark night, I knew that it was wrong, but I did it anyway. I had never been to his house. I barely knew him. But go I did. It had been weeks and I wanted to get high.

Once there, he lit up the pipe and kept talking and smoking and talking and smoking. I sat and stared at him like a dog eyes someone who is eating, hoping they will drop a morsel of food. I didn't hear anything that he was talking about but nodded my head at what I thought were appropriate moments. Eventually, he handed me the pipe, put a new rock in, and lit the fire. Relief flooded my body as I took in a long, deep breath, the water bubbling and the freebase filling my lungs. He took the pipe from my hand and set it on the nearby table and I slid to the floor, my back resting on the sofa as he came to collect his prize. I was so sickened by my behavior that I never did drugs again after that. Disgusted with myself, I vowed to get clean.

The next morning, I called in sick. I told myself and my family that I had the flu and I went to bed. I took Advil and I stayed in bed all day. For several days after, I tossed and turned and sweated it all out of my system. It took weeks for my energy to return.

It would be two years before I could see someone using freebase or heroin on TV or in a film without having the physical reaction that I'd had when I used it before. It really had a hold on me. If people were smoking crack or freebase on a TV show and I heard the sound of the bubbles in the pipe or saw the smoke, I would have to get up and run to the bathroom. The physical hold on me was still that strong. I feel very fortunate that by the grace of God, I'm still alive. There were so many times I could have injured myself or others while being high. Or simply not woken up. But, by the grace of God, I got clean and filed for divorce.

How quickly life can change. Only a few months after hitting rock bottom, my divorce was finalized and I was untethered and unattached. I was sober. I felt happy. I felt free.

Now free of drugs and free of Amir, I was back in the routine of my work as a legal assistant for a real estate attorney and family life taking care of my stepson.

After all that I'd gone through, I felt much older than my 27 years, but I was still young and single, and I was filled with hope for my future. Before long, a senior partner at the law office began to pursue me.

His name was Tom. He was a beautiful man. Smart, funny, positive, handsome (a Kris Kristofferson look alike!), generous, ethical, loyal, and kind to everyone. All of the attorneys were nice to me and flirted with me, and Tom was no different. And, per my usual, he was married. But, one day, when he asked me to get a drink after work, I said yes.

We went out and talked about a lot of things, including his wife. He was pretty cut and dried about it, saying that he'd been married for 20 years and there was nothing wrong in his marriage but they had become like brother and sister, and he wanted more. So, we casually met for drinks and conversation until the day he told me that he wanted to be with me and that he was leaving his wife.

It turns out they had had an open marriage for a while and she already had another boyfriend, so he didn't feel that guilty. It had been a long time since he had experienced love like this and he wanted it in his life. He was 40 and I was 27—classic. Tom was honorable. Tom was a saint. He loved me. He was proud of me. He respected me. He stepped up. He was a lovely, lovely man.

I didn't think I could find happiness like this. Amir was in jail. I was alone with Bijan. I did not know anyone who would date me with a small kid in tow. But Tom did. He wooed us both. I loved that about him. It was VIP seats at the 1984 Olympics, Dodger games, ski trips, miniature golfing and horseback riding trips, and his law firm picnics. Bijan and I could not help but fall for him. He was a classy guy and he wanted me all the way.

In one of our early talks, I told him that I did not feel that attracted to him because we were too similar in our coloring. I always went for tall, dark, and handsome—edgy or foreign—anything different from me. But Tom was tall and blond (salt and pepper gray), and I didn't feel those butterflies with him. I wasn't used to the feeling of calm and peace I felt when I was around him because I'd never known a functional relationship and didn't recognize it.

"It's okay," Tom said. "I have enough attraction for both of us."

We had been living together for a year. Tom had bought us a beautiful contemporary home in Newport Beach. It was large and open, with high ceilings and lots of large glass windows overlooking the ocean and Balboa Island. Bijan was in school and I was working at a retail chain in their real estate department. Life was good. We were settling into becoming a family unit. Tom was doing everything he could to make Bijan feel comfortable and welcome.

It was a Saturday and the three of us were driving to a Dodgers game.

"You're gonna love the Dodger dogs," Tom said to Bijan. "And we have great seats," he added, trying to impress.

"My dad has taken me to lots of baseball games," Bijan said, scrunched down and hunched over from the tiny backseat of Tom's new red convertible Corvette, another perk of his newly single status.

"Oh, that's great," Tom said. "Did you enjoy it?"

"Yeah!" Bijan said.

"Cool," Tom said.

Stepfather was a new role he would need to navigate. He had a new job title, new young girlfriend, new house, new car, and new life.

We rode for a while in silence, and then Bijan leaned forward and asked, "How tall are you?"

"Oh, let's see," Tom said congenially. "I'm 6'4," why?"

"My dad is seven feet tall," Bijan said, and Tom and I exchanged glances.

In Bijan's young 11-year-old mind, he could see and appreciate Tom's success, which clearly impressed him, but he was reluctant to show it out of loyalty to his father.

We were trying to play happy family and Bijan was thinking about his dad in jail. It was a reality check. This was a very hard time for him.

But, I was determined to move forward. I had left Amir and that life behind me. Tom and I were building a life, and it was good.

It was Christmas and Tom's parents were visiting from Indiana. His dad was a doctor and his mother was a very smart and accomplished teacher. Both were very conservative and kind people. It was important to Tom that they approved of me. We were getting ready to go out to dinner; Tom, in his black slacks and crisp white shirt with a red cashmere vest, sat on the end of the bed and reached for my hand. He was such a nice dresser, and at 6'4" everything looked good on him. I was equally dressed to impress in my black cocktail dress and pearls, and I let him take my hand as I moved closer to him.

"Merry Christmas, love," he said, as he pulled me into a close embrace.

"I love you."

"I love you, too," I returned, and meant it. When I was with him, I felt comfort and ease and friendship, and I was happy around him. Safe. Looking back now, this really was the first relationship that I'd had that made me feel secure and cared for. This was a healthy relationship. Suddenly, Tom turned his head, raised his voice, and called out to Bijan.

"Bijan, can you come here for a minute, please?"

Moments later Bijan ran into the room.

"Yeah?" he said, looking at Tom and then back at me quizzically.

Tom stood in front of us both and slowly bent down on one knee before us.

"Deborah and Bijan," he said. "You make me very happy and I want to build a life with you both. Will you marry me?"

My mouth opened, but no words came out. Tom held up a red box with the lid open, revealing a gorgeous, huge pear-shaped diamond ring set in gold with large diamonds on either side of it. It was stunning. I looked at Bijan and he smiled broadly at me and nodded his approval.

"Of course," I squealed, looking at Tom.

We were officially engaged. Tom pulled me in for a kiss and hugged Bijan and me together in a warm embrace. Then, walking out of the room grinning like a kid on Christmas, he said, "Let's go tell everyone."

"Mom, Dad, she said yes!"

Tom told me later that he had asked Bijan beforehand, in private, for his permission to marry me and Bijan had said yes. His feelings for Tom were confusing to him because of his loyalty to his father, but their bond would remain steadfast and strong for the rest of their lives.

I was 30 and Tom was 42 when we married. We had a beautiful wedding and an amazing three-week European honeymoon. He did everything first class because he wanted to show me how much he loved me. Being with Tom gave me prestige. Being married to the senior partner at the top law firm in LA gave me credibility. I'd never had that. It felt good. However, since when had I ever been content with what I had?

* * * * *

I was driving home from a full day of looking at potential properties for my client, a growing photo chain. My thoughts were on my upcoming wedding and finding my wedding venue. Most traditional venues waiting lists were a year out, so I needed to find something out of the box. Tom wanted a big wedding because he'd not had one the first time around when he married his college sweetheart, and I certainly had had a less than memorable wedding when I donned my Jordache jeans and eloped to Las Vegas.

While I was stopped at the light on Newport Boulevard, my gaze wandered to a charming Spanish architecture building. What struck my eye was the beautiful courtyard that had a tranquil fountain behind huge iron gates and the stunning, dramatic, matching staircases that started on the second floor and curved and met at the bottom. The building was gorgeous, with stunning marble floors. I was filled with excitement.

This is it! I thought to myself. I could see myself getting married there. The only problem was that it was a bank and financial plaza, not a wedding venue.

No problem, I thought, ever the optimist.

I will just work my magic.

I jotted down the address and drove home to call the number of the leasing office. This was the perfect location only a short distance to the 55, 405, and 73 freeways and Pacific Coast Highway. My guests would have no trouble finding it. Several phone calls later, I got a callback and informed the office that I'd love to rent the facility for a wedding.

"We don't rent out to weddings," the uninterested girl on the phone said.

"But I really need this location," I implored. "We can do it on a Sunday and we'll be in and out. Please make an exception."

Much pleading and name-dropping later, they agreed. It was a magical wedding complete with white doves released at the end. Many guests said it was the most beautiful wedding they'd ever attended.

* * * * *

The guests were finishing their dessert and coffee. I had changed from my beautiful wedding gown into my white lace mini dress, and joined my new husband so that we could greet our guests before leaving for the honeymoon.

"You are a beautiful bride," Tom said, squeezing my hand as we walked table to table, engaging each guest in conversation and thanking them for coming.

"I love you back," I said to my new husband, proud of him and excited about our future together.

"The limo is here, time to go," Tom said and headed in the direction of the door.

"Okay everyone, on your feet, the happy couple is leaving! Let's give them a warm send-off," the MC said.

There was a gauntlet of guests and we were led down the path where they all threw rice and flower petals at us. Holding hands, we ducked and laughed and ran to the limo where our parents were waiting to kiss us goodbye. My mom was taking care of Bijan and Tom's parents were heading home. We got into the limo and breathed a sigh of relief.

Tom and I arrived at the Bradley International terminal and found the gate from which we would be leaving for Paris. We boarded the Pan American airplane and headed to the first-class cabin.

"Welcome to PanAm," the attractive flight attendant said as she guided us to our seats.

"Would you like champagne?"

"Yes!" we both said at the same time and laughed. We were so excited to be going on our three-week European vacation with destinations in Paris, Rome, Amsterdam, and Sweden. This was the first time out of the country for Tom and his travel agent had laid out our itinerary in a very detailed manner.

We left on Monday morning and arrived in Paris on Tuesday morning. After making it through the health, immigration, and customs formalities, we headed to baggage claim and met our representative, a well-dressed man with a sign that read "WELCOME – JOHNSONS." We got into the beautiful black stretch limousine and settled in while he chatted amiably, pointing out sights on the way to our beautiful suite at the Hotel De Crillon.

"Good morning, Mrs. Johnson," my husband of 24 hours said.

I giggled and kissed him on the lips.

"Would you like your coffee on the terrace?"

"Absolutely, Mr. Johnson," I said and walked into the

bathroom to find the most scrumptious white terrycloth robe and put it on. I handed the larger one to my handsome husband. We sat on the terrace enjoying our strong *café au lait* and fresh croissants and wondered how things could get any better.

We spent the morning touring Paris. We saw the Place des Pyramides, Tuileries, and Louvre, and went to the Pont Neuf, Notre Dame Cathedral, Latin Quarter, Sorbonne University, Luxembourg Palace and Gardens. We visited the Invalides, the Eiffel Tower, the Arc de Triomphe, and several churches.

That evening we enjoyed a delicious dinner on the Bateau Mouche along the Seine River. The sites along the way were all lit up beautifully and romantically. It was the perfect way to spend the evening. We went home to our bridal suite for dessert.

This was day four of our honeymoon and we had been running on adrenaline. The jet lag now hit us hard. We took a car to the Palais des Arts Modernes and the Bois de Boulogne to Versailles. This beautiful 17th- and 18th-century palace with its chapel and famous Hall of Mirrors was my favorite stop. The gardens held such charm for me with the mazes and statues. I think I had lived a previous life here.

We had a beautiful outdoor lunch at the Restaurant Pre Catalan in Bois de Boulogne. Once lunch was devoured and accompanied by a delicious bottle of Bordeaux, we spent a romantic afternoon in our gorgeous room.

We spent the next three days traveling by train down the coast. We stayed in Nice at the beautiful Negresco Hotel. We shopped and ate and slept and just honeymooned. I put on my cute outfit of shorts and a cropped top that we had just bought along the walkway and headed down to the beach. I threw the towel that I'd brought from my room directly on the sand and lay face down, prepared to read the book I'd brought from home. Tom was sitting face up in a chair next to me.

"Uh, honey," he said in a halted voice. "You might want to take a look at this."

"Huh," I said, putting my book down.

I lifted my head and looked at him, and then moved my eyes to see what he was looking at. All of the women were topless. This was a shock for us. We giggled and tried not to look like tourists. I laid back down on the towel, removed my top, and then untied the swimsuit top that was underneath it. I felt so decadent!

"Turn over," Tom said, laughing. For the briefest moment, I got brave and turned over topless on the beach! Of course, when in Rome (or Nice), right?

After lunch, we toured the Grasse perfume factory, went to Cannes and shopped some more, and toured the yacht-filled harbor around Cap d'Antibes.

This was a very enjoyable end to France, and now we were off to Milan.

It was the day after my birthday. I was 30, married, and in Italy. I had to pinch myself. We were staying at the beautiful Hotel Excelsior Gallia. It was an opulent suite and I felt so pampered.

We spent the day walking around the small shops and had dinner in our room.

"I have a surprise for you today," Tom said.

"What is it?" I asked excitedly.

"You'll see. Come with me."

We walked outside the hotel and parked in front was a cute dark green Alfa Romeo convertible that Tom had arranged to be delivered to the hotel for us.

"Get in," he said.

"Where are we going? Do you know how to drive over here?" I asked him nervously.

"Sure," Tom said, smiling. "There's nothing to it."

We got into the small Alfa Romeo with the top down and I pulled my hat down tightly on my head, channeling my favorite actress, Catherine Deneuve. Tom pulled out a map that the concierge had marked up for us.

"You navigate," he said.

"Oh, wow." This was going to be an adventure. Surprisingly, we made it in one piece down the Autostrada, through the Po Valley, passing Parma and Modena, to arrive in Bologna and to our hotel, the Royal Carlton.

"What are we doing here?" I asked.

"Well," he said, "since it's your birthday, I wanted to get you something special. We are meeting my client and friend Luiggi Pascal. He owns a fur factory."

"What?" I said. "No way!"

"Yes way," Tom said, so pleased with himself. "We are meeting them now for lunch, and then after lunch, we are going to his factory and you are going to pick out any fur you want."

"Oh my God," I said, kissing him. "You are the best husband in the world."

"I know," he said.

We met Tom's friend, Luiggi, and his beautiful wife, Gianna, at an outdoor restaurant high on a hill overlooking the charming city. There were terracotta rooftops for miles mixed with lush green mountaintops. It was a wonderful afternoon. We ate, drank, laughed, and then walked through the town together, tasting a gelato from a sidewalk café. This was a scene out of a Sophia Loren movie. Truly surreal. We ended up at the nondescript door of a three-story building.

"Come in," Luiggi said, unlocking the tall metal door and guiding us in. We entered his private office and the walls were lined with pictures of smiling people in fur shaking Luiggi's hand. Luiggi guided us down a hall and into a large room with racks and racks of furs, with gold gilded mirrors positioned along the walls.

"Take a look," he said, extending his arm toward the pelts and coats on the wall.

Pouring over the rows and rows of furs was overwhelming. After an hour of looking and trying on delicious fur coats with Gianna's help and guidance, I settled on a white floor-length mink that I loved so much I could have named it. Needless to say, I was thrilled and very appreciative. Tom was treated like royalty that night and it rivaled a scene out of a James Bond movie.

We left early the next morning, setting off in our little coupe through Ferrara with its old Renaissance atmosphere, and continued to the ancient Roman town of Paua, known for its art treasures and university, before finally making it to Venice.

We traded in our car for a boat taxi and motored over to the beautiful Hotel Danieli. This was a stunning hotel on the water, looking majestically at the city. What a view our room had. After lunch, we took a motor launch to the Island of Murano for a visit to the glass factory and the Cathedral at Torcello.

The next morning, we woke up and had breakfast on our private terrace and then took a walking tour with our guide, Mo. We began with St. Mark's Square and viewed the various monuments like the Basilica. I loved chasing the pigeons and making them fly up all around us.

Mo showed us the private canals and residences that other tourists did not get to see. My favorite was the Doge's Palace, the luxurious residence of the ruler of the former Venetian Republic. We toured the doge's private apartment and the Great Council Hall with beautiful paintings placed on the ceiling, which you needed a mirror to see. We saw the old prison and the Bridge of Sighs. We spent our last night together with an evening gondola ride in the romantic atmosphere along the Venetian canal, with musicians serenading us. It was breathtaking.

"Come on honey, time to get up," Tom urged.

"Man, this honeymoon stuff is tiring," I said, and we laughed.

"We need to hurry and be at the Santa Lucia Station by 11 am," Tom said. "We are taking the Orient Express back to France."

"Oh, wow," I said, excited.

"Yes," Tom said, reading to me from the itinerary.

"For nine decades, following its maiden journey in 1883, the Orient Express carried diplomats, royalty, smugglers, and spies…until its final run in 1977. Now, this famous train has been restored and runs again. Your meals on board will be prepared by skilled chefs and served with finesse in the mahogany teak-paneled and brass carriages."

Tom was in a tuxedo and I was in a black velvet knee-length dress with gold braids and large jewels decorating the bodice. We made a stunning couple, and people noticed us wherever we went.

"Happy?" he asked, as we drank our after-dinner port. The chef was preparing our bananas foster and the flames from the fire were getting dangerously close to my hair.

"So happy!" I replied. "This has been an incredible trip and I will never forget it."

We traveled on this amazing train and chatted with the other passengers, who were from all over the country. This iron steed continued through Verona, Innsbruck, and Zurich while we slept in our private sleeper car until the morning, when the conductor said, "Paris—our final destination."

* * * * *

We had now been married for six months. I was happy. Life had gone back to its normal course. Tom, Bijan, and I moved to a new home in Newport Beach. We had a beautiful view of the ocean overlooking Balboa Island. We were a happy family. We were all three excited about the move to Orange County, which offered us a fresh start. With Tom's encouragement, I started my own company and I was again representing retail chains in their real estate expansion.

Tom and I began to socialize and often had parties at our home. On one of these occasions, our friends Steve and Marie brought another couple along. They were a cute couple and we all became fast friends. Eli was in the clothing business and wanted to open his second retail store. I wanted his business, so I contacted him a few weeks later and asked him to meet for lunch. I remember it like it was yesterday.

We arrived separately at the restaurant. I was waiting at the table and Eli walked in quickly and sat down. We exchanged pleasantries and ordered our food. I made my pitch and requested to be his exclusive broker in finding new locations for his store.

"Why should I hire you?" he asked.

"Well, I've represented many national tenants and have many great contacts. I also know the market very well and will act as your real estate department so that you can focus on the retail business," I finished.

He looked at me for several minutes, saying nothing, and then,

"I'd like to see you on a regular basis as friends with benefits."

"What?!?" I said. "You're married."

"So?" he said.

"No!" I said.

Just then the waiter set our food in front of us. Eli got up from the table without a word and left. As I sat there, stunned, I watched him leave the restaurant. This is the classic scene in the movies where the girl usually leaves and the man hastily pays the bill, only in this case, it's me throwing down money and jumping in my car as he pulls out of the driveway.

I am reasonably intelligent and well-balanced. I have a good job with a good income, and I am considered credible and trustworthy. However, if a man shuns me in any way, I become completely derailed, trying to win his love.

We were each driving down the Coast Highway in the same direction. He had left the restaurant in a hurry, leaving me to pay the bill. I could not believe his rudeness. I pulled up beside him, rolled down my window and said, "What the fuck?"

He motioned with his hand for me to follow him, and I

followed him off the highway into a beach parking lot. It was early afternoon and deserted. He got out of his car, walked directly over to the passenger side of the car, and, without a word, slid into my car, took my face in his hands, and kissed me long and hard on the mouth. Time stopped. For once, I was speechless.

Not to sound like a cliché romance novel, but from that point, it was on, hook, line, and sinker. I was newly married and completely obsessed with another man.

It was even more terrible because he and his wife were friends of ours and we did a lot of socializing together and saw each other often. It increased the intensity between us because on occasions when we were at the same party, we didn't interact with each other. We would mingle and connect with other guests while being super aware of each other, and we knew how to tweak one another delivering alternate pleasure and pain.

Since returning from the honeymoon, Tom had gone back to the business of being the senior partner of a very busy, top law firm. He worked long hours, leaving the house at 7 am and returning at 7 pm. I was lonely. I was 32, immature, and needed attention. I had my own business and I had a lot of free time to do what I wanted. When someone showed me attention, that was what I wanted.

I pushed the button on my mobile phone that dialed Eli directly. "It's me," I'd say,

"How's your day?"

"Good," he'd say. "Busy."

"Meet me for lunch," I'd cajole sweetly, dying for a distraction from my day of calling tenants and trying to get a deal done.

"Can't," he'd say shortly. "Have to work."

"I got us a hotel room right up the street. Surely you have an hour," I'd say enticingly. This was me trying to pry him away from his work to focus on me. I was relentless and the daytime was my safest time when no one was looking for me. It was the opposite for him. His family worked with him and he was not invisible.

"Okay," he'd say. "One hour."

"Great," I'd say happily. "Meet me at the Best Western just down the street."

Eli and I began sneaking around during the day once or twice per week, getting a hotel room, and then socializing in a group with the spouses at least once on the weekend. He was Israeli, and I was drawn to his olive skin and jet-black hair. He had piercing green eyes and he had been in the army. Hot. He was smart, charismatic, and driven. He was an entrepreneur.

What I didn't know was that his ambition led him to want what Tom had, namely, a hot blond on his arm. His wife was short and Israeli. Very nice, very cute, but not the tall American blond that was the status symbol he craved. The relationship continued. My friends knew. My mom knew. I was in so much angst over this. I was obsessed.

Tom did not seem to notice. He was a very even-keeled individual. Eli, on the other hand, had issues. I later realized that he wanted me more because I was Tom's wife, rather than loving me for myself. Men envied my husband. They wanted what he had. My husband was tall, good-looking, respected, and had financial security. He was a top attorney. I fit Eli's criteria for feeling that he had accomplished something if he could make me want him. He felt this gave him power over Tom. I had never dreamed of this. This guy was possessive and we were continually fighting about who I looked at and who I talked to. This was a volatile, intense, explosive affair that was to become the ruin of me. He told me from the beginning that if I left Tom, he'd dump me. I did not understand it. It was getting harder and harder to remain at home in my shell of a marriage, when my heart longed to be with Eli.

After two years of carrying on this affair, I could not take the deception anymore, and I did leave Tom. I moved out and got an apartment. Eli was beside himself, and then I understood what he meant. It meant that I was able to be out in the world as a free agent and he wasn't. He could not take that. He began to distance himself from me. He wouldn't return my calls. I felt he was cheating on me. He was a master manipulator and a liar and I had seen him in action. It ripped my guts apart. I learned that there was an older woman that he had been involved with from day one and continued to see. He had a connection to her because she was one of the first women he met when he came to America, and she helped him get started in his business.

I'm sure he loved her. I saw blood. I was furious. I was so possessive of him.

One day, not able to keep this pain to himself, Tom called Eli's wife and told her that her husband had been cheating on her with me. She immediately kicked him out of the house and he got an apartment.

Once the truth came out, I knew that I had to tell our friends before they heard it from their husbands. My book club was that night. I told them what I'd been up to and read them the apology letter that I'd written to Eli's wife, my friend whom I had betrayed. My friends were shocked and outraged. They did not expect this of me. It was the farthest thing they could imagine. I was banned and they did not want to see me. I had no support.

Both of our divorces imminent, Eli and I tried to have a normal relationship with each other, one that wasn't shrouded in secrecy and sexual tension. I started visiting him at his new apartment. He had two little girls. They were both sweet and super smart. I'm sure the divorce was very hard on them, but since they knew me and liked me already, they were happy that we were together. We fell into a relaxed routine. We would cook dinner together at night.

When we made rice, I would put a pat of butter in the water to boil. This is the Iranian way that I'd learned from Amir. But it's not the Israeli way.

"Why don't you commit to me?" I asked one night after dinner.

"You put too much butter in the rice," he answered, only half kidding.

This became a metaphor for my life. I've always done things in a big way. An over-the-top way. I'm certainly no shrinking violet. Since he would not commit to me, we broke up and each got divorced. He began dating a girl who worked in a department store. I was devastated. I thought he loved me. He lived with her for two years. I felt so rejected and used. I felt like damaged goods. I had thrown my life away for a fantasy.

The experience was so horrific that, for years, just seeing Eli's company name in print made me feel physically ill. This man had ruined my life and my reputation. He was a despicable person and I wanted to be as far away from him as possible. To make it worse, his retail business had grown from the four stores that I helped him acquire to having 240 stores nationwide and a net worth of $45 million. Life was not fair. I could not cover my overhead and he was driving Bugattis in Monaco. But, how can I blame this on him when I was a willing participant? Why did I still feel like that little girl on the outside of the window with my finger pressed to the glass, watching everyone else live their best life?

For so many years, I held onto the idea that he ruined my life. My weight ballooned and I went into a very dark depression. I started isolating and could barely focus on work. I begrudged him all of his success. Each time I saw him, I would turn and walk the other way. There was never a clearing or an apology from him. Just heartbreak. My world fell apart. I had lost my marriage. I had lost my friends. I had lost my family and my integrity. I was lost and needed help.

By some miracle, I found Howard M. Halpern's book, *How to Break Your Addiction to a Person*. This book saved my life. I learned about attachment hunger: "Attachment Hunger is the basis of being addicted to another person." I discovered that the degree to which we connect with a person in a relationship depends on the level of gratification we received from our parents in the attachment phase of our life, and whether they allowed us to become independent around one-and-a-half years old in the launching stage.

Attachment Hunger is a situation that replicates the experience of our childhood. As an infant, if we were not held and shown the love and acceptance we needed, we would long for this as adults, and in each romantic relationship, we continue to try to get this love and approval that we so badly long for.

Even when our mothers do a great job of meeting our needs in the attachment phase, our fathers must help us separate from our mothers and step in to help us gain autonomy. This is the launching stage, a crucial step in an infant's development. If this doesn't happen, the child will have the propensity to be clingy and needy, feeling addicted to their parent and subsequently to their partner. I didn't have this important launching.

It wasn't Eli that I loved. It was the familiar experience of rejection, which set up an uncontrollable craving for him that I continued to pursue but could never reach. Each time I would try to leave the relationship, I physically felt that I was going to die. Since there was no father present when I was an infant, I did not have the experience of being taught to detach from my mother in a healthy way. As a result, I continued to either hold on too tightly in a relationship or not at all.

This is what makes love sometimes feel like an addiction. As a love junkie, I would say or do anything to get my fix. I was constantly looking to find that love that would make me feel seen and safe. It took me a very long time after Eli to heal. But with time, I took a risk again and found a partner that was loving and stable. But addictions are a tricky thing—when we start to overcome one, another rears its ugly head.

My early childhood trauma caused me to feel unlovable, and this was a hole that I'd be trying to fill my entire life. I never felt good enough. From the time I found out that Ron was not my father, I struggled to find my self-worth. I did not know who I was and felt that I did not belong anywhere. I was a bastard (in those days the word had meaning) and an orphan.

As I grew, I struggled to find my worth. My value. I never felt that I was worth much, and I believed that my father left because of me. He and I struggled. We were always in one conflict or another. He didn't like my grades, he didn't like what I wore, he didn't trust me, and always checked up on me, I cost him too much money. So, when he and my mother broke up, I felt I was to blame.

* * * * *

I was in Las Vegas for my annual ICSC (International Council of Shopping Centers) convention. I was in the hotel lounge when I saw the name on the TV screen.

"Turn it up," I called to the bartender, and heard a newscaster report, "Michael Anderson charged today with life imprisonment without the possibility of parole."

The background noise in the bar faded away. I was frozen in my tracks. I could not believe what I had heard.

He did it again, I thought. The feelings of that day all came rushing back to me. The pain. The shame. The disappointment. Back in high school, there was a favorite outdoor hangout area called Red Rock Canyon that all of the kids went to. The story was that a woman rebuked him and he killed her. Guess, I was lucky.

CHAPTER 6

Growing Up

A fter a time, I healed from my adulterous relationship with Eli and remarried.

This was my third marriage and might have been my healthiest relationship. James and I were equals and true partners in every sense of the word. It had been ten years since my last marriage, and I had grown up a lot since then. I had been clean and sober the whole time and was ready to have a family with this man. I had seen Bijan through college and he was successfully living independently, as an adult. James had brought two sons to the marriage who I loved and happily co-parented.

We stayed married for 16 years and we did our best. Unfortunately, despite both of us wanting it to work, this marriage also ended in divorce. Our relationship was fraught with dysfunction. We were either very happy or completely shut down.

Even after months of separation, I wasn't sure that we should divorce. I still loved him and was still attracted to him. We felt comfortable together. But everything had changed. James was angry. Nothing I said or did was right for him. We'd been living different lives for a very long time. The pressure of life and making money got to us. We were in survival mode and going through the day-to-day motions of trying to maintain the lifestyle that I wanted.

After the divorce, I asked myself, What have the last 16 years been about? What is my future?

There were so many unanswered questions. The future had become quite scary for me. I was now 50 and I feared that I would never get it right in a relationship. I worried that I would be alone forever.

With my happily-ever-after no more, I asked myself, "What now?"

I think it is fair to say that I wallowed for a bit, cried, walked around like a zombie, listened to country western songs, ate too much, cried some more, and kept the world at arm's length. But just for a short while. I knew that God had a plan for me. James needed to leave to fulfill his destiny and I needed to let him go to realize that I did not nurture and appreciate him the way I should have. We were both mirrors for each other and we were what the other needed for the time we were together. Sixteen years was a milestone. It is my longest relationship and I was faithful. It was important to me to keep the commitment since I had not in the past.

After my divorce, I could not imagine kissing someone else or being attracted to anyone else. James had so many good qualities that I loved. His looks, obviously, his sense of humor, his loyalty, his kisses, his beautiful green eyes.

Sixteen years of history and mementos, gone and now irrelevant. The pictures, the cards, the memories—what to do with those? The man I'd been with for the last 17 years was gone. It felt like a death in the family. I was so used to seeing him everywhere and having him to talk to and make decisions with and share my life with. Now I was alone and family and friends didn't know how to comfort me. They felt that since it was a decision I'd made, I must have wanted the divorce and I could just move on. To some extent that is true. It was a decision I made, but the aftermath of the feelings is very hard to deal with. When the holidays rolled around, I no longer wanted to host these occasions. Family gatherings in the past had often been at our home. But now, it was so much harder being the only one to plan, shop, decorate, cook, host, socialize, clean up, and put everything away. I just was no longer motivated. It felt like my arm had been ripped off.

The analogy of divorce being like a death in the family captures the profound impact that divorce can have. Both experiences involve significant loss and require a period of adjustment and healing, but society responds very differently to each.

When friends and family lose their partner or spouse

via death, I feel their pain, but, conversely, they do not seem to feel the weight of the pain I felt going through my divorce. I sometimes wanted to say, *Hey, losing a husband through divorce is hard, too.*

On the emotional side, both divorce and death involve a sense of loss. With my divorce to James, I lost not only a partner but also the hope of a shared future, a daily routine and vision of what the future was supposed to be like. This left me with a deep sense of grief that felt like a death had occurred.

Just as the death of a loved one can shake one's identity and place in the world, so too can divorce. I needed to redefine myself, navigate life changes alone and navigate the emotional feelings of failure having gone through another divorce brought up.

There was little support for me. Like others dealing with losses from death, I too needed emotional validation. I needed to find a core group of people who would listen, offer compassion and understanding so that I could process the loss and move forward.

Joel Osteen and Joyce Meyers got me through this difficult time. I found comfort in listening to him in my car and it was so helpful. I would watch Joyce Meyers on YouTube in the mornings as I got ready for work. Her daily message was always spot on for my life. It was amazing how she always said what I needed to hear.

These teachings began to take hold of me. I wanted to be a better person and a better partner. I didn't know if I would get another chance at love, but if I did, I vowed to do it differently.

Going through this last divorce with James made me much more aware of my emotional fragility and gave me a deeper compassion so that I can help others going through divorce feel less isolated and more understood.

* * * * *

Back home, I got on with the business of life. It was two weeks before my divorce was to be final. I'd been alone for seven months and was doing fine. James and I attended the wedding of his son, and each of us was comfortable being there together, him with his new fiance.

I was keeping busy with my ranch, where I had three horses and three dogs. My life was in order and on track and I was hopeful of the future. I believed that I was exactly where I was supposed to be, according to God's plan.

CHAPTER 7

Love or Limerance

Newly single and curious, I had recently discovered Facebook. I began looking up friends from my hometown. I decided to look up my college boyfriend, Raymond. After a few clicks of my mouse, I was staring into the eyes of my long-lost love. Another one that got away. He was dressed in a tuxedo, looking as handsome as ever. It looked like he was a successful photographer now. I sent him a private message and told him I'd be in Las Vegas in a few weeks and asked if he'd like to get together for coffee.

A few days later, my friend Deb and I were getting mani-pedis, laughing and talking about nothing in particular. Unexpectedly, I felt the phone in my lap vibrate, and when I glanced down at it, I did a double-take. I could not believe my eyes when I saw the name on the screen. I gasped. The text said he was in shock to hear from me. He said he had tried to find me for years and thought I was dead. My eyes filled with tears as I continued to read. My friend was still chatting away in the chair next to me, oblivious that I'd been struck by lightning.

This changed everything. For the next 24 hours, I could think of nothing else. I was transported back in time to 30 years earlier when he was mine. Mine as much as he was anyone's. Raymond was a young hotshot engineer living in another city in the same state. He worked at a leading electronics company, winning award after award for his cutting-edge injection mold. His sister was my co-worker at the Dunes Hotel in Las Vegas, and she had set us up on a blind date. There was intense chemistry. He was 6'2" with gorgeous green eyes and very smart.

Unfortunately, back in the day, we were too young to settle down. From our first meeting, I fell instantly in love. He was everything a girl dreams of: tall, handsome, intelligent, drop-dead gorgeous. He was smart, sexy, and confident. He knew what he wanted and he was on track to get it. He preened and spread his feathers and I was helpless under his spell and would do anything for him. What we didn't know at that time was how brief our time together would be. We traveled some, and we even brought each other home to meet their family. He taught me to ski, gave me my first camera, and taught me how to use the dark room.

But, we were not meant to be at that time. He lived in

Reno and I lived in Las Vegas. Neither of us wanted to relocate. I was on a fast track. I was 20 years old and ambitious. Growing up in Las Vegas, I had been sheltered from the fast life of the Strip. Now on my own since my parents' recent divorce and my mother's subsequent departure with her latest husband to another state, I was trying to learn to support myself in an unforgiving town. Young and beautiful, and feeling invincible, I was oblivious to the dangers of being a young girl on her own in a cold, hard town like Las Vegas. I was fresh meat and the natives were restless.

Suddenly, I heard my friend's laugh and was jolted back from thoughts of the past into the present. Here sitting with my feet soaking in the warm bubbly water, I continued to read his text that said he was shocked to hear from me and was so happy I was alive. He had worried because when I had called him in those early years after leaving Las Vegas years ago, I'd obviously been high and he was concerned. He said he'd often wondered where I was. He went on to say that he had spent hours on the internet trying to find me, but could never pick up a trail.

We began to text back and forth. It was 2014 and the iPhone had just come out, and texting was new to me. I remember the thrill of seeing those moving dots dancing on my phone promising his attention and love. The delicious feeling of being seen.

Raymond was a night owl and I had a day job, but that didn't stop me from behaving the way I did back in the days when I would stay up all night doing coke and then going to work the next day. Instead, this time, I was texting Raymond. We would start communicating around 9 pm and text until about 3 am, and then I'd get a few hours of sleep and get up early to go to work.

He was love-struck too, yet being a left-brain engineer, he was much more analytical than me and questioned this feeling. Even though we both were certain we had been struck by a thunderbolt, one day early into our reconnection, he asked me, "Is this love or limerence?"

"What is limerence?" I asked and immediately began to research online. I read pages and pages of articles I had downloaded. An infatuation.

American Psychologist Dorothy Tennov coined the phrase Limerence in the '70s. In her book *Love and Limerence*, she describes the physiological effects of intense limerence can include shortness of breath, perspiration, and heart palpitations. If there is extensive anxiety, incorrect behavior may torpedo the relationship, which may cause physical responses to manifest intensely.

We were both definitely feeling these responses!

As M. Scott Peck describes in his book, *The Road Less Traveled*, Limerence is the heady feeling of intense longing for another person even when they don't fully reciprocate.

You don't forget your first love. And we had unfinished business. The feeling was so strong that we both questioned this love, or perhaps this limerence, yet we both continued happily down the road to find out.

We made plans to meet in Las Vegas in a couple of weeks. Before the visit, we spoke on the phone and Raymond explained his living situation. As it turned out, although he was not married, he was involved in a long-term relationship with a wealthy woman. He had met his girlfriend, Candace, 30 years earlier when he was 30 and she was 45. She and her husband owned many hotels on the strip and had a very lavish lifestyle. Candace took a liking to Raymond and did the full court press to make him hers even though Raymond was married to another woman at the time. He and his wife had just had a baby and yet he left his new family to hook up with Candace. They traveled the world and entertained celebrities. Although she was devoted to Raymond, Candace never made it legal. She never divorced her husband because she didn't want her kids to lose their status or money, so Raymond publicly became "the friend," or the escort. Yet, he did everything for her.

Now, all these years later, we have reconnected, and he was re-thinking the decision he'd made those many years ago and questioned whether he'd made the right choice. His present relationship had waned, which gave us time to explore what it would mean to be together.

I checked into the opulent room on the 24th floor of the Caesars Palace. In town for a work convention, I put my clothes in the closet and could think of nothing but him. It had been 30 years since I'd seen him, and although I hardly remembered our time together, he was in my DNA. I was dying to see him.

I opened the door and he walked in, passing me. I was trembling and practically gyrating with excitement and anticipation. I reached out to him and pushed him against the wall.

He was visibly nervous.

"Sit down," he said, taking my shoulders and guiding me to the bed. He wanted me to back off—I'd invaded his space and he wanted to control the situation. We moved to the velvet sofa situated in the large suite, overlooking the lights of the city where it all began.

Facing each other, our eyes locked—he was so near that I could smell him. I breathed in the thick, wonderful aroma that was him. I was an inch away from him, then a half inch, his face so close to mine.

"Don't move," he said and came a millimeter closer until I could feel and breathe in his silky mustache, a strange sensation I'd not experienced in 30 years. His lips on mine, we connected, and I felt him as naturally as if I'd been kissing him every day for the past three decades. A perfect fit. He's holding my face, exploring my mouth gently with his tongue, deeper and deeper as the memories refresh and download to the monitor of my mind.

We had a very strong soul connection, but we never got to be physical life mates. Our love was interrupted by geography and distance and life events. But through it all, we came back and found that we still had the same feelings for each other, but again, it was not meant to be.

After it was all said and done, I don't think it matters

whether it is infatuation or love. When it's mutual, it is a coming together of two souls who see each other. We were both so energized from the thrill of knowing that the people we were in our youth still wanted the people we were in our maturity. We still had the hope and the dream that we could come together and make our story work. He had always wanted marriage. The solidity of a family. I wanted connection, love, and commitment. A partnership with someone I loved. Raymond brought the passion out in me. He often reminded me that I made him feel loved, appreciated, and seen. He loved the attention I lavished on him.

Although Raymond and I were aware that this was infatuation, we proceeded with abandon anyway, eyes open. A computer whiz and photographer, he began to send me all of our old pictures that he had kept from 30 years ago. I could not believe he still had them! The pictures showed it all. We were in love and we made a beautiful couple. Just as he still had our pictures, I had kept all of his old letters and pictures, too. Seeing him again brought all of the old feelings back.

And through all of this, mostly built upon memories, we fell madly in love and wondered how we could reconcile this in the present day. He was very attached to his lifestyle and had no financial means of his own. I was financially comfortable but had no long-term security and was nowhere near the means of his present partner. He awakened in me the passion and electricity that I was starving for and never thought I'd feel again. His mind was a perfect match for me. He once was mine, but now was with someone with very deep pockets. I could not compete.

Raymond didn't work. Candace was his job. He was her houseman, chauffeur, videographer, and PR manager. Although he was once appreciated, she was now tired of him. He stayed, hoping she would do the right thing, but she wasn't free to make a commitment to him. She was still married. Raymond resented that he had given her 30 years of his life and had put his own life on the back burner. Now, he had the thought of me on his mind and the "what if" and "if only." But, I quickly saw that he could not commit. He could only ruminate. He was an analyzer, and not so much a doer.

Not wanting to jeopardize his lifestyle and security, we decided to shut this down before it began. Once again, our love was not solidified.

We never stopped communicating. We tried to be just friends, but although not physically acting on the feelings, my heart continued the affair with faith, perseverance, and hope. I was sure that he was my forever love and that we would be adding to the love story we started so many years before.

My divorce had shattered my confidence, but now, with Raymond's love, I began to learn how to love myself. It felt good to be wanted again and my confidence grew. I began to ask for help and to expect more from others. I learned to let someone reach down and pull me up, and in the end, that was what was needed. I learned to love and accept myself, healing the old shame that had haunted me for years.

Raymond sent me different email addresses to use and changed the passwords often. He wanted to be very discreet and cautious. He was quite the IT wizard. I was enamored with his technology skills. He was my ground control to Major Tom.

One day, he upped the ante and gave me the passwords to his home security cameras. I was depraved enough to use them. I had front-row seats to their lavish parties, his office, and their kitchen and dining room. It was a 14,000-square-foot home and they had 13 dogs! This was my new obsession. My evenings consisted of sitting in bed with my laptop in front of me, watching Candace at her dining room table playing solitaire with him sitting across from her watching TV, both obviously comfortable with the other as any 30-year partner would be. They would exchange pleasantries of the day and interject their political opinion of the newscaster's latest story. I had put my life on hold to become a voyeur of someone else's.

One night, after Candace had gone to bed, Raymond was alone in his office at his computer. He stood up and adjusted the camera so that I could see behind him. The screen was filled with rows of black bins with yellow tops. Large 100-gallon bins. Raymond said there were 100 of them and he needed to go through them before he could leave. This was 30 years' worth of possessions that he had collected and carted around. For the first time, I began to understand what I was dealing with. He was exhibiting a true hoarder mentality.

"I just have to go through all of this stuff and then I'll be out of here," he said.

"No, problem, I have a 40-foot shipping container," I said, trying to entice him.

He said he wanted to leave. He wanted to be with me. He just needed to sort some things out first. Like what to do with all of these bins. I began to lose hope. I could see that he was never going to make a change. It was too hard for him. Even though he was not happy, he was comfortable.

Several months later, I was stunned by the words I heard him say.

"I'm ready," he said. "I'm on my way."

I could not believe it. He had packed up his beautiful black Escalade that had been a gift from her, with his dog, Chip, and had left Candace a note. He was headed my way and I could not be more thrilled.

It was 12:30 am and I was waiting in the parking lot of the closest market to my house. I'd suggested we meet here so that he would not get lost trying to find me. As I saw his headlights approaching, I took a deep breath and tried to quell my nerves.

"You made it," I said, sounding more jovial than I felt.

"Yeah," he said, hugging me. "Long drive." We kissed briefly and jumped back into our cars for the 12-minute ride home.

"Follow me," I said and kept my eyes glued on his car behind me, determined not to lose him after wanting him for so long.

"Welcome to mi casa," I said as he pulled into my drive and got out of his car.

"Wow, it's dark out here," he said, looking around and I wondered what he must be thinking seeing my 1,500-square-foot farmhouse compared to his opulent mansion.

I helped him unload a few things, led him to the guest room and closet, and showed him where to put his things. We had a beautiful first night and a fun second day. When we got home from our dinner and movie—our first real date in 20 years—the phone rang, and it was Candace. Raymond left me alone and went to my guest house to take the call. When he returned an hour and a half later, he announced he was going back. The next day, true to his word, he packed all of his things up, put them back in his car, and returned to his safety net. Tears streaming down my face, I watched incredulously as his car left the driveway. I never saw him again.

If it wasn't over before, it certainly was then. I was dealing with a child and I did not want to be his mommy. I wanted a partner and I wanted a happy ending. Maybe I was unrealistic.

This felt like déjà vu. Back in the day, when we were together in our twenties, Raymond had not been ready to settle down with me. Now, we were at the same crossroads we had been then, so many years before. He was still not committed. I needed to move on. I will always think of ours as one of the most intense relationships of my life.

Our (non)affair became so frustrating. I wasted so much time settling for crumbs. My relationship with Raymond lasted two years and it wasn't even a relationship. It was a fantasy on both our parts.

Looking back, once I took the blinders off, Raymond's responses were giving me a clear message. When he said, "Oh, you are so over the top," or, "You give me a lot to think about," his words were a pushback, like cold water on a fire. Someone should have slapped me like Cher slapped her boyfriend in the movie *Moonstruck* when she said, "Snap out of it!" He was stalling. I should have listened and believed him. It is not the same as if he were to hold me and whisper, "You are my destiny and I am yours—don't move—I want you. I'm going to do whatever it takes to get you." He was not mine to want. Yet, I allowed him to continue dangling the carrot. It felt like I was on a roller-coaster ride of "… maybe, maybe, maybe … then the abrupt halt … stuck on the tracks … then the car rolls backward … then forward … and the ride is over." And then you get off the ride and you walk down the road and think, *That ride was too short, maybe I should go on it again.*

If you've read this far and you just finished the last chapter, which was all about my crazy menscapades and failed relationships, you might be asking why I am writing another chapter on love. Limerence?? Cathexis?

When not in a relationship, people with love addiction

issues can feel normal and sane in other areas of their life. However, once they enter a new relationship, they suddenly find themselves in an addictive cycle again.

When Raymond came back into the picture, I had had three years of sobriety from my primary addiction, food, which I will discuss in the next chapter. I'd been clean from sugar, flour, and alcohol, and I thought I had it all together.

After having had a 16-year marriage to James with no cheating on my part, not much drama, and no drugs or alcohol, why did I fall back into a crazy, drama-filled relationship? I thought I was healed from this obsessive behavior.

I had so many thoughts rolling around in my head at that time, all triggered by this one man:

After only four months into this journey with Raymond, I can see the connection to addiction. The first few months were filled with adrenaline, and I felt alive and full of hope. The physical reactions are quickened breathing, dilated eyes, and sexual feelings in my body. It is just like being high.

If you have an addictive personality, that addiction is always waiting for a chance to rear up again and take you down.

After a few months, the physical intensity subsided, and instead of being in a euphoric state, I was like a heroin or meth addict still in search of the drug. I was tense, jittery, anxious, and in search of my next fix. I needed it badly. The problem was that this time, the drug did not work as it had in the beginning. I needed more—I needed constant reassurance—I didn't get the same feeling and was constantly looking for evidence that he felt the same.

There was no way that we could continue on the same path or we would crash and burn. Raymond recognized that, but I did not. I was oblivious. My addictive personality wanted more, more, and more. When I'm in this state, I am panicked and I am very, very manipulative. I will say anything to avoid appearing needy, so that I can get the reinforcement I need. I am passive-aggressive—I try to withdraw to appear in control. I complimented him, I cajoled him, and I sexualized every conversation, trying to appeal to his male side. When I don't see a need in him, I get panicked—I don't know how to manipulate him if I don't know what he needs.

One of my friends said it best: "You don't take lovers, you take hostages."

Even as I actively pushed a man away, I would try to get him to swear his undying love to me. If they still loved me after I constantly tested their commitment, it was proof that they loved me. Before Raymond was around, I wasn't missing anything. I was content and happy—full of hope. Now that he had become my new addiction, I was just full of hurt and angst.

I needed to get him out of my system, so I could stop wanting him. I had to give him up, to end the cycle of love addiction.

Finally, the pain in this relationship got so bad that I

needed help. This was affecting me in a very negative way. I was beginning to isolate and my mental health was threatened. I couldn't work and I couldn't sleep. One day, I was desperate for help, and I looked up *love addiction* online and was directed to an SLAA meeting.

The woman on the phone directed me to an in-person meeting taking place later that day. Finding the address and pulling my car into the parking lot, I made my way to the little room in the back of a church. *Randomly, I wondered if Sex and Love Addicts Anonymous was available years before when I'd had the destructive affair with Eli.*

Embarrassed to walk in, I slowly pushed the door open, afraid that I would find a room full of degenerate men who sit in dark movie theaters and jerk off, but I was in so much pain that I went anyway. As I entered the room and sat down among the group, we went around the circle and I heard my story. People just like me were in pain over their relationship. I learned that Raymond was my drug, they called it a "qualifier," and I needed to cut off *all* contact. I turned off my phone that day and began counting days. I am more than my possessions and my looks. I have a huge heart and a loving spirit. I am enough. Why is it so hard for me to believe? People want to love me but I don't let them in, choosing instead to be around people whose love I need to win. It is more comfortable for me to be with someone else who shares the belief that I am flawed.

* * * * *

The silence is deafening. Now I understand the meaning of that phrase. It's funny how we don't understand certain phrases we have heard our entire lives until we experience the circumstances that make the meaning crystal clear. Now I get it. It had been 4 days and 23 hours since I sent Raymond my last text, ending it all. The one that if I went back on it, I would be reducing my credibility with him and myself. My text said, "Raymond, I want to do the right thing, so it's over between us. It just has to be."

Did I mean it? No! But I had to do it.

Do I wish he'd say, "Don't go…" Yes! But this time my declaration is met with silence. I credit his silence to the fact that I told him I was out of money. He heard me, and he believed me. And it was true. *It was important to me not to be involved with someone who was not free.*

But that didn't stop me from wanting him. Each time we tried to break it off, I could not breathe. I needed to stop obsessing and completely freaking out. I was staring at the phone—willing the next text to come in.

This is no way to live. I can't do this to myself. I had been sober in my 12-step food program for three years, and I could feel myself getting pulled off-center. I began to pray. *Lord, how do I treat myself with love and respect? Please take away my difficulties so that victory over them will show others your power, glory, and love. Lord, I want my soul mate. Do I deserve him? Is it my time love-wise? Have I earned that right? Probably not, but I know that you love me and want the best for me.*

My definition of happiness is wanting what you already have. It's like wanting a Ferrari or a Gucci bag—if you want it and you can't afford it, you are in lack and in pain. It's the wanting that gets you in trouble.

Men and money have been tainted for me my entire life. I've never had enough of either. I've always been wanting for more and am envious of others who've had it. More love, more money…my life could be defined by me being addicted to "more."

So, I check my phone every five minutes, and then I check my email. In the past, he made sure that every day his name showed up on my screen either by text, phone call, or email. But now he is doing the right thing. *Wait,* I think to myself, desperate to connect with him*, there is one little crack that isn't shut.* That is the video cam that I still have access to.

So, I quickly grab my iPad and click on the icon that gives me access to his house. Nothing happens. I watched as the circle on the screen just turned and turned. But it does not open. I feel sick to my stomach. *What is happening? Has he changed the password?* I can't breathe.

I check my Wi-Fi—it is on. *Why won't it open?* The need I have feels exactly like the nights when I was out of coke. The last of the rocks had been smoked and it was 6 am. I was crawling on the floor, combing through the shag carpet, looking for MORE. The metaphor for my life. I have gone through everything I have, and I want MORE.

The withdrawals of this romance were brutal. I was

edgy and sick with need. I was putting on an act and going through the motions of being ok, yet I remained desperate for him. Desperate for my phone to ping and tell me that he needs me, too. That he was also bereft, and to live without me would be impossible. All I've wanted my entire life is to be loved and to feel secure in the knowledge that I was enough, yet here was another reminder that I'm not worthy.

After two weeks of no contact, I got strong enough to delete the camera apps from my laptop that tied me to him, making it impossible for him to text me. I went cold turkey. It was empowering and gave me relief because now I could stop checking my phone every two minutes.

Today is day 21 of no contact, and I no longer have the fantasy that he will leave her and come to me.

Although he couldn't text me, I hadn't blocked his email. He kept emailing me pictures of where he was in the world on his two-month European excursion. While I found his actions insensitive and hurtful, I had a personal hand in my self-inflicted pain. It made me sad that there were no words attached to the images he sent. I wanted to hear that he was miserable and that he wanted me and only me. However, that was not the case. He wanted us both. He wanted his stable life and he wanted the excitement of knowing I was out there loving him and giving him lots of attention.

I wanted that, too. An attention junkie, I missed the texts, the pictures, the emails, the calls. I missed it all. I longed to know that he cared about my movements and thoughts during the day.

I'm so far into this addiction. Co-dependency or emotional love addiction. I am hooked on Raymond. He has left me. He had the strength and courage that I did not. I see that he chose to stay with her. He is staying. Why is that so hard for me to see? I thought that he loved me. I can't seem to find someone who will choose me and stay with me.

I'm lost now. The little girl who's been abandoned and feels ashamed because she's not good enough. I'm on the edge. I'm reinforcing all of the things that are wrong with me. I have tools, I can turn this around. The first thing is to be present. To ground myself in my surroundings. I'm in my office. Both feet are on the ground. My three dogs are next to me. I have people who love me. I have animals that count on me.

I am activated right now by his lack of attention. I am the little girl who is waiting for her mommy to come pick her up at school and she is late. I'm vulnerable, exposed, and worried.

It was time I asked myself the hard question: What was I holding on to? A memory from my past. A sweet wonderful warm memory of a time when I was full of hope, love, and energy. I loved him. He was the first person I had felt this way about since James, 16 years earlier. He was my rebound.

He woke me up. He turned me on. He loved me, and I

felt loved. I felt adored. I always put more value on what others have. If I had valued what I had, maybe I'd still be married. Do I regret the divorce? Do I want to go back? No.

When I'm in my addiction I am absent from all things life. I am not able to see what's in front of me. I am far, far away. I am dead. I am in pain. I am dulled. I want to be left alone with my pain. Maybe I'm addicted to the pain. Self-pity and self-centeredness—those are my character defects.

When I don't have a man to attach to, I feel so empty. I feel irrelevant. I want a partner who sees me so that I can feel alive. Validated.

Our mothers always told us to find someone who loves us more than we love them. They are probably speaking from experience. I have always struggled with this concept. I have been with two people who loved me more. While it felt good, I seemed to have abused the privilege.

When I know I have power over someone, I seem to use it, or more specifically, abuse it. It is only when I am feeling that desperate feeling of longing for another that I equate it with love. That strong challenge of needing to win someone's love defines my whole existence. I seem to have entered this world with an agenda that I will make "THEM" love me.

Maybe the lesson that I will finally come to learn is that I came here to find self-love and self-acceptance. I have always been the first to blame myself or take responsibility for problems that arise. I let others off the hook and blame myself. Self-flagellation at its finest; that's what I do. I start the dance over so many times. I say that I am done and then I continue. I waste so much time. Why do I allow it for myself? I need to step away and be a better parent to myself. It is time. Life is short. I've done okay. I've paid my dues and I'm a hard worker. I deserve someone who will make my life better and commit himself to being a help, not a drain.

My partner must be free and unencumbered physically and emotionally! That is the bare minimum. When I'm in this state I let everything affect me. I am weak and vulnerable. Co-dependent. Why do I allow this to happen? I must shore myself against this and do something to counteract these occurrences.

Action and meditation are what work for me. That is what I need to do. Stretch and meditate. Free myself from negative self-talk. I'm okay. I'm a child of God and I deserve love.

As for Raymond—he is a sweet memory. A scar, really. I still have a mark on my heart. But, there is a mark there reminding me that it was a cancer that needed to be cut out. It has been a long, hard, painful experience with only a few rewards. I hit the bell a few times and got the little prize. I never won the jackpot, and if I did, what would that be? That I would get to support him financially? Then, I would lose respect for him. But, I don't want to end up bitter. He was very loving to me the entire time. Our reunion was a monument to our past, to our youth, when things were carefree, and a reminder of our vibrant and virile past. That's all. He has a place in his life with comfort and security (to a point). That's all most of us have really. Just for today.

Limerence is a funny word. The feeling that it evokes replicates love, but isn't. It is only the promise of love that matches the image we have created in our minds of what love looks like. Real love is more like what M. Scott Peck describes as "oatmeal love"—the kind of love that lasts the test of time. The love that continues through sickness and health.

One of my life coaches, Pamela Deneuve, taught me that everyone has a BOP (Basic Operating Principle). Together we discovered that mine was, "I am damaged goods and I don't deserve love and happiness." In her book, *Healing Heartbreak,* she explains, "This principle was behind all of my actions and life choices and it was running my life." Even though I am bright, attractive, and self-supporting, I never felt that I was worth much and I still held the old belief that my father left because of me.

Pamela taught me to LAUGH when Raymond would say "I love you" and "I miss you." I needed to change the feeling it evokes from pain to ridiculousness. To see the absurdity, because in my world, if you want something you can have it, and if you don't want it, you say, "No thank you," and it's best not to want something bad for you.

She helped me to stop holding on to destructive relationships and using them as an excuse to feel bad about myself. Raymond decided to discontinue contact. That is what I said we needed and I wanted. He is only doing what I told him to do. Now, I am getting something out of feeling sorry for myself. I'm allowing this to make me feel like a piece of shit. Very old, very familiar. This is replicating a historical event.

As I continued working with my life coach and love addiction sponsor, I began to see that my character defects are comparing myself to others, coming up short, beating myself up, feeling that I need to try harder, and thinking I don't have what it takes—that I don't quite "measure up."

In reviewing this very unhealthy attachment to Raymond, I realized that I can't be with someone who is so secretive. That is a red flag. It brings up adrenaline—something old and scary. I don't want to be the secret, like I'm illegitimate.

Addiction has caused me to make poor choices. By acting on my feelings, I have made so many mistakes in my life. God has given me many good men. I have had two good marriages. I ruined them both. With Tom I was unfaithful, and with James, I was critical and I gave up. I did love him. I was faithful. Now, reading our old cards and letters, I believe that he loved me, too. So sad. What a waste.

I was turned on by the narcissistic, unavailable man who offered a challenge and replicated the childhood angst I felt by not having a father figure as an infant and then having an ambivalent, immature stepfather who did not express love to me.

I'm not ready for a relationship. I'm going to make a relationship with myself. I'm going to take an inventory and see if I'd want to be in a relationship with me.

This was the point where I began to heal. I put down the drug and stepped away from our relationship, which had no integrity. I surrendered to God and asked for the craving to be taken away. I deleted the apps on my laptop that were the portals to the cameras to his home and I stopped going to the hardware store for milk. I plugged back into my life and started anew. That is when I decided to move forward in a positive direction—I chose joy!

CHAPTER 8

Hungry for Love

I've been hungry my whole life—hungry for more. *More* was my mantra. Moderation was not in my vocabulary. If one was good, five were better. Especially, when it came to food, alcohol, and men.

I'm six years old and I'm in my living room. I'm pulling the chairs from the dining table one by one, into the living room and arranging them facing together. Next, I take the pink chenille bedspread from my twin bed, drag it down the hall, put it over the top of the chairs, and crawl inside the dark, safe cocoon. I'm alone. I wish my parents would get up soon. I want them to play with me. See me. Love me.

The silence is interrupted only by the loud, singular ticking of the clock. With each click, click, click, I crawl out of my cave to go into the kitchen to find a friend. I find it on the Formica counter. Quiet as a mouse, I open the soft rectangle package wrapped in shiny white plastic covered with balloons and promising Wonder. Carefully, I remove two pieces of the soft, fresh, white bread and return to my sacred fort. My little hands squeeze the bread into two balls and I bite into the comforting, gummy, textured dough and chew and chew and chew while I wait and wait and wait. As the minutes became an hour, I retraced my steps to the kitchen many times and repeated the process of squishing the soft bread into hard little balls and eating them, determined to fill the emptiness inside me.

Weekend mornings were the time my mother would attempt to appease my stepfather for the baggage that she brought into the marriage—namely, me. They would spend the mornings alone behind closed doors. This was the time I was expected to fend for myself and leave my parents alone while they slept in and reconnected from the long work week. Food and the TV were my only comfort and solace.

I was a latchkey kid, as they called it back in the day, returning home alone after school and letting myself in with the key hidden under the potted plant at the front door, doing chores until my mother returned from work. Eating and watching TV alone until right before they were expected home, I would tear through the house, emptying ashtrays into trash cans, cleaning toilets, making beds, and throwing dirty clothes into the overflowing hamper. Then, once my mom was home, it was time to prepare dinner, and the happy family would gather around the table and talk about their day. But those memories weren't so happy. Food wasn't a comfort then. I would listen to the bickering going back and forth at the table and the angry silence that followed it, and I did not want to eat. I had lost my appetite. Yet, I was forced to sit there until my plate was clean. So, sit I did, alone, after they had left the room, leaving me with three-quarters of a plate of barely touched stuffed green bell peppers and peas that even the dog wouldn't eat.

Food has always been my go-to. I've eaten when I'm hungry. I've eaten when I'm not hungry. Happy, sad, nervous, and depressed, food was always the answer for me. In my early years, the food did not show on my body. I was blessed with a high metabolism and I was a skinny kid. However, with puberty and birth control pills, my body and my breasts exploded. Everything I ate stuck on my hips and my stomach. This was a problem I did not know how to handle. But, of course, my girlfriends did.

"Take this pill and you won't be hungry at all," they instructed. The good news about those pills is that they curbed my appetite and they made me want to clean my apartment. The bad news is that after all that housework, I could still eat.

* * * * *

"Hi, I'm Deborah, I know I'm fat…"

It was something I would blurt out within the first few moments of meeting someone. I wanted you to know that

I knew I was fat and I was trying to do something about it. It was my default to announce my condition immediately upon meeting you. I've had body issues my entire life and have always felt huge.

When it comes to FAT, that three-letter word conveys so much. So much shame, so much loneliness, so much pain. Even when I wasn't alone, I was lonely. I tried so many diets. Thinking back, the first and best cure was the drugs of the '80s: the cocaine diet. That worked well. The freebasing all night, the heroin chaser, and the lack of sleep really did the trick. I was thin. Very, very thin. But as they say, "Thin is not well."

When my then-husband got arrested for selling cocaine to an undercover cop, I decided it was time to get my act together. I could not end up in jail because I was the daughter of a cop and that would be embarrassing to my family. So, I threw away all of the freebase pipes and I flushed the drugs down the toilet and I began to get clean.

As my husband did his time in jail, I did mine at home alone. Since he was my pusher and I did not have another drug connection, I took to my bed, tossing and turning with the effects of a wicked drug withdrawal, and kicked the habit cold turkey. It took about two weeks of telling myself and my friends that I had the flu to sweat it out, and little by little, I got clean.

As I began to regain my health and become myself again, my next suitor came into the picture. This was in the form of the senior partner at the law office where I worked.

He was smitten. Dumping his wife for me, he began to woo me. Now drug-free, I began to enjoy those fancy restaurants where he was putting on the full-court press. Drinks, appetizers, bottles of wine, desserts, and aperitifs began to take their toll on my size-six frame. It was back to trying to control my weight and white knuckle it. I was losing this battle.

Once we were married and the white wedding dress had been put away, the pressure was off and so was my resolve. The weight began to return. I came to learn that the fat, in addition to being a symptom of eating too much, was also doing its job in another department. It was meant to keep everyone away, especially my new husband. The loneliness and insecurity of my childhood made it very hard for me to let him close. I needed this fat suit to keep me safe. Because being thin for me meant being vulnerable. Being sexy was scary.

I did not know how to communicate without feeling sexualized, or maybe it was me doing the sexualizing. I don't know, but it was very uncomfortable. I've hidden behind my fat for years. This pattern repeated itself many times. I would be thin, get a guy, balloon up, and test him to see if he really loved me. If he stayed, there was something wrong with him; if he left, he's an asshole. I push people away because I'm afraid.

It had been years since I'd used drugs, and alcohol was just something I used for fun that I enjoyed. I said that I didn't have a problem. I liked to drink socially, and I did not get drunk. The alcohol didn't change my personality like it did for those angry women who became ugly when they drank. It was just fun, and everything was good until it wasn't. I began to see the pattern that a) I could not have just one drink; and b) I could not eat moderately if I drank. The sugar in the alcohol made me crave other things. In addition to sex, mainly carbs (vast amounts of bread and pasta), but also, afterward, pints of ice cream. Then came the concoctions I needed to put together, and finally, the list of ethnic foods I needed to eat. My mind was so busy thinking about what I was going to eat next. I could not concentrate on you or what you were saying. I could not remember your name, but I could tell you every restaurant we had eaten at in the last five years and what both our meals had consisted of. *Oh, you have breast cancer. I'm so sorry…those crab enchiladas are really good, aren't they?*

As they say, admitting it is the first step. I began to see that I had a problem. I had hit bottom. The deciding factor came one time when I was preparing to make a meal for myself. It was my Friday night ritual of pasta, wine, and chocolate chip Haagen Dazs for dessert, consumed while watching the two movies I had selected from the corner Blockbuster (yes, this was before Netflix). The water had come to a rolling boil on the stove and I had just poured the entire box of linguine into the water. I was filled with anticipation. I was content.

Then, my serenity was rudely interrupted by a knock at the door. I answered it and found, to my extreme chagrin, my stepson standing at the door. He thought he'd surprise me. He was so proud of himself, thinking he was doing something really sweet, and all I could think was that he was interrupting my precious ritual of eating alone— stuffing myself and falling asleep watching TV. I was pissed. He was confused. Needless to say, that evening did not end well. I'm ashamed to say I did not invite him in. I told him I was expecting a guest and he needed to call next time. Yes, this was a new rock bottom for me. I was fat, angry, and alone.

Once I gave up drugs and alcohol, food was what I used to fill the hole inside of me. It became my drug of choice. I used food to avoid my emotions. To avoid feeling uncomfortable I would continue to stuff myself until I felt sick.

My favorite foods were heavy, greasy, starchy foods that reminded me of things my grandmother made for me, like tuna casserole, rice, spam, and pancakes. Mostly white flour products and carbs. Food was a comfort to me, a constant and faithful friend. It filled me up when I was lonely, anxious, or afraid.

That is how things were until one day over a decade ago, I realized that I had had enough. Enough of being a victim. Enough of letting my life pass me by. Enough of killing myself slowly. When I'm in the food, I am miserable, desperate, and scared. More importantly, I am in pain. Flour and sugar cause inflammation in my body and I literally can't turn over in bed without pain. Walking is difficult, too, because my knees begin to hurt when I ingest sugar.

In due time, I was ready to change. Ready to surrender. Surrender to the concept that alone I could do nothing, but if I could ask for help from a higher power and believe that that help was possible, I could make a change.

I admitted that I was powerless over flour, sugar, and alcohol.

Today, I have my life back. I began a 12-step recovery program for food in 2003 at age 48, weighing 220 pounds. This amazing program has given me discipline and structure in my life. Today, I weigh 145. It's because of this program that I have maintained a 75-pound weight loss for over a decade.

Before the program, I held myself back in my life by not having discipline. I often quit before I accomplished my goals. By being weak and prone to giving in to immediate gratification, I weakened my opinion of myself. I couldn't trust myself. I have always had very little self-discipline because I thought being spontaneous and going with one's feelings was more fun. What this meant was that I didn't get to learn the lesson that every action has a reaction or a consequence. I never looked past the NOW to see what price I would have to pay or what I would gain if I just stayed abstinent. But now, one day at a time, I feel stronger. I work hard and put in the effort. I have a positive outlook. I know that I can do anything I set out to do if I just stay abstinent.

Men, money, and food are what I've used in the past to soothe and comfort myself, and now I have tools that I can use when the cravings come up. It feels wonderful to be in a healthy body today and to no longer hurt myself with food. There is a solution!

CHAPTER 9

Broke Not Broken

When I wanted to buy something, I generally did it without much thought.

I often ran out of money before I ran out of month. I've made large amounts of money in my lifetime, and yet it slipped through my fingers like sand. There never seemed to be enough to sustain my lifestyle.

How could I be out of money? I thought to myself, I still have checks!

I remember the time I showed up in our driveway with a new Cadillac Escalade. I had a road trip with clients planned to show properties and felt certain that a bigger car would benefit me greatly. Without hesitation, I drove to the nearby Cadillac dealership and left an hour later with a beautiful champagne-colored Escalade complete with a gorgeous moon roof and tinted windows. Driving home, the new car smell of leather was intoxicating. As I pulled into our driveway, my husband James, who was in the front yard watering, turned toward me and mouthed, "What the fuck?" eyes bulging and eyebrows raised. His face said it all. He was not happy, especially since I had not discussed it with him.

"This is our new car," I said. "Isn't she beautiful?"

"Are you crazy?" came his reply.

I don't consider myself frivolous. I use money to pay for things I need and things I want, but invariably I continue to find myself where I started: broke, tapped, and in arrears. There was never enough money to make me feel safe. When I got the money, I felt wonderful; Powerful, safe, and secure. But it was always short-lived. When the money ran out I felt shame. I felt like a loser.

What is wrong with you? the voice in my head would berate me. You can't hold on to money!

I'm not a drug addict. I'm not blowing it on designer bags and jewelry, I would justify defensively, talking back to the voice. But still, time after time, the money was here today and gone tomorrow.

If an idea for a party popped into my head, I would begin the planning, preparation, and spending right away. Being spontaneous gave me a rush; I loved the adrenaline I'd feel. I'm impulsive, often jumping into the proverbial pool before checking to see if there is water in it. When I wanted something, I would put it on a credit card and figure out how I was going to pay for it later. It always worked ... until the bill showed up.

I pulled into the public parking structure on Bedford Drive in Beverly Hills. The traffic had stressed me out some, but it was early afternoon, so it wasn't too bad. I was early and still had plenty of time to make it to the meeting. I parked my car in the public parking structure and began walking the short walk south to Wilshire Boulevard. As I passed shop after shop along the way, my gaze was fixed on the beautiful and enticing store windows. I was imagining how I'd look in each outfit and admiring the backdrop of the window designs. At the corner, waiting for the red light to change, I noticed I was outside the Prada store and saw the SALE sign in the window.

Ooh, I need some retail therapy, I thought. It was 30 minutes before the meeting and it was only a short walk away. I had time to kill, so I let myself be drawn into the store. I'd recently earned a very high six-figure commission check and had always wanted a Prada handbag. The impeccably groomed salesgirl welcomed me in and began to point out the features of the latest bags of the season. Before long, I found one that I liked on sale and happily told her to "wrap it up."

In just a few minutes, I walked out feeling much smarter and more successful with that gorgeous designer bag on my arm—and yes, $1,200 poorer.

Looking back, I can only surmise that I must have been feeling insecure about the upcoming meeting. In those days, I was not very good at understanding my feelings or even looking at them. At the first sign of insecurity or anxiety, I would medicate myself by eating, drinking, or shopping. In this case, I found myself lured in by the shop window telling me that relief was inside. I believed that walking into the meeting with a name-brand bag on my arm would somehow validate me. I used to intentionally put on the jewelry that I had received from my second husband when I had an important meeting, broadcasting to the room that I was affluent and worthy. Adorned with all of those large diamonds, made me feel competent and powerful. Yet, the first thing I'd do upon returning home after work would be to remove my designer watch, rings, bracelets, and earrings. I didn't need my armor at home.

Weeks later, I arrived in Las Vegas in the late afternoon for my annual work convention. I had haphazardly thrown my clothes and makeup into my suitcase at the last minute, barely making the flight. I have such anxiety around packing that I leave it to the very end and most of the time do not take what I need.

After a quick flight, we landed and as I walked toward the baggage claim, I noted that the cocktail party was in one hour. This was a valuable networking event and the invitation is included in the convention admission ticket. As I anxiously watched the carousel go round and round, waiting for my luggage, my apprehension was growing.

I did not bring the right clothes—I don't have anything to wear to the party, I said to myself.

Okay, I thought, I'll stop by the Fashion Show Mall and quickly find a blazer.

The cab driver stopped in front of the entrance to the mall, opened the trunk, and retrieved my suitcase. I handed him 30 dollars in cash and he drove away. The double doors automatically opened and I walked inside, pulling my inadequately packed luggage behind me. I walked into shop after shop and could find nothing. As the clock ticked, my frustration grew.

What was I going to do? It was 8:50 pm and the store was about to close. At the last stop, my eyes landed on a powder pink cashmere Chanel blazer. I tried it on and it fit me like a glove. It was beautifully tailored and understated. I had missed the party but this would work nicely for my 9 am meeting tomorrow. I looked at the price tag and was shocked to see $900.

Wow, I thought, *this is more than I've ever paid for an article of clothing.* It was not in my budget, yet I heard myself say, "I'll take it," handing over my groaning credit card to the sales clerk. This is my famous Chanel blazer story and is a reminder of what my inability to plan and pack accordingly has cost me.

When I have money, it feels so good. I am a Good Time Charlie. I want to spend my money on myself and others. But when it's gone, the feeling of emptiness comes back. There is no better feeling to me than knowing there is enough money in the bank to pay my bills and to have something left over to feel secure.

My family was middle class. Both of my parents worked full time and I worked and was required to pay for anything that I wanted that was extra. Clothing was extra. My stepfather didn't think braces qualified as essential and sadly my husband got saddled with this when I was in my 30s. The same applied to college.

Since my first job at 15, I have always worked, but I invariably spent more than I made. That left me vulnerable and at the mercy of people, I might not otherwise have given the time of day to.

I've had vast amounts of money. One year, five years ago, my annual gross income was $800,000. I bought my mom a house and paid cash. I've owned a Mercedes, a Porsche, and an Escalade. But then, within two years, I'm usually back to where I started. This is a recurring problem.

"God, why does this keep happening to me?" I'd wail, sitting at my desk looking at the stacks of past-due notices. I was not ready to believe that it had anything to do with my actions.

I've heard it said that "Why" is not a spiritual question. Instead, I had to turn within and ask myself and God why these patterns kept repeating.

What is it that I am doing that brings me back to this point of being broke? What lesson are you trying to teach me that I haven't yet learned?

So, I guess a better question is, How? How am I sabotaging myself? In the 12-step program, HOW stands for Honesty, Open-Mindedness, and Willingness. I needed to look at the actions that kept me in this terrible hole.

It has always been easy for me to spend money. I like my creature comforts, cable TV, fine dining, cleaners, Sirius XM radio, nails, hair, riding lessons, etc.

When I'm feeling anxious, it helps me to have things in order and tidy. It quiets my mind and calms me and I feel more in control. I like a clean home. I'm attracted to beauty. Having a beautiful environment makes me happy, and this costs money.

I'm making it my mission to warn women that we must get solvent and protect ourselves for the day that we do not have the money we need to continue the lifestyle that we've become accustomed to.

SOLVENCY
/ˈsälv(ə)nsē/

noun
1. the possession of assets in excess of liabilities; ability to pay one's debts.

Being solvent means having enough money to pay for all of your debts. It doesn't mean stressing out to make more money, it means living below your means.

BE SOLVENT TO BE HAPPY

The number one problem I hear from women in my

coaching practice is economic insecurity. They cannot afford themselves. They don't make enough. They don't have enough. They need someone to subsidize them. When we can't afford ourselves, we make ourselves vulnerable to others. We jeopardize our integrity. We give away our joy because we compromise what we want to do or be.

Owing more than we have or earn can weaken us. We need to strengthen our foundation. Let's go back to the beginning and back to our roots. Let's strip away all of the fluff and rebuild our house stronger, brick by brick. Where we are wasting money that would be better spent in our own pocket rather than given to someone else. This is a process. Let's look at every aspect of our lives and see where we went numb. When did we stop being in charge of our money? When did we stop being good stewards of it?

I asked myself: *What is the lesson I need to learn? What can I do today to be more solvent?* I can spend less. I can delay gratification. I can sell what I own, decrease my spending, AND increase my earnings. Even when you know what to do, it isn't always easy to do it. I am still trying to learn this lesson.

It is said that most of us are about two paychecks away from being homeless. I do not have a paycheck. I rely on commissions from real estate deals I make. What happens when there are no deals? Or the money we are owed is delayed or doesn't come? If the seller reneges? What then? Have we protected ourselves from possible pitfalls? I never did. I always thought there would be more. Like a faucet—the money would just keep coming.

In her book, *"It Takes Money, Honey,"* successful businesswoman, Georgette Mosbacher warns, "The only person you can depend on to take care of you financially is...*you!!!*"

This smart, ambitious woman grew up in poverty, helping to raise her three younger siblings while her grandmother and mother worked to keep the family afloat after her father's death. As an adult, divorces from two powerful men left her financially and emotionally bereft, while a split from the former Cabinet Secretary Robert Mosbacher rocked her world yet again.

In her book, Georgette demonstrates how to create a financial safety net so you will never be caught short in a crisis, whether from the loss of your job or the loss of your husband.

As women, we wake up one day and realize we are alone. There is no one coming to save us. There is no prince on a white horse riding in. Divorces happen. Husbands die. Sometimes in the case of a second marriage, you expect you will be taken care of financially when your spouse dies, but his adult children have other ideas and you are given a year to vacate the home that you shared with your deceased partner.

We can feel we are safe, and then an unforeseen circumstance occurs, and we are stuck. Money is never a sure thing. It comes. It goes. We have to learn to live on less and be happy. We must plan ahead for pitfalls or droughts. We can't keep doing what we've always done expecting a different result. Let's all say it together: "That is the definition of...yep...insanity."

Our choices and actions determine our outcome. Did we fail to protect ourselves? Did we fail to set aside money or save for a rainy day?

I was recently in a situation that called for legal action to force someone to pay me what they had agreed to. Unfortunately, I did not have a legal fund and could not afford an attorney. Also, I did not get a proper agreement signed upfront. I could have protected myself in the lease agreement, but I didn't want to rock the boat and I trusted that the people involved were honorable, so I thought it wasn't necessary. These circumstances were all in my power to correct, to take care of myself. But I didn't. So, the outcome is on me. We need to take responsibility for our actions.

As I looked at my character defects, I saw the actions I took that weakened me. The actions that left me vulnerable. These were my choices. I wasn't bad. I wasn't good. It wasn't a moral issue. God gave me free will, but the consequences were not free. My life situation was the result of my actions and they had a price.

I had a very hard time delaying gratification. It felt boring to think about tomorrow. I wanted what I wanted when I wanted it. Each decision boiled down to I deserve this, I'm entitled to that, and I want/need it now. My self-centeredness was in full bloom.

I acted out with men, money, and food addictively because I didn't want to be uncomfortable. For me, any emotion made me uncomfortable. Also, it was hard to ask for what I needed, because I didn't want to make others uncomfortable.

I have a difficult time getting in touch with my feelings. When I am stressed or anxious, I eat too much, spend too much, or act out, so that I can get relief instead of processing my feelings. If I took the time to look at what I was feeling, I could begin to understand the fear or loneliness I was feeling. When I make an extra purchase on the credit card and then tell myself I will cut back tomorrow, I am kidding myself. I need to be a good parent to myself through the urge. I need to PAUSE. It stands for Pause Action Until Serenity Enters.

How many times have we taken for granted getting a manicure, going for sushi, getting a massage? How about lunch with the girls? A birthday present for your bestie? A bottle of wine? No money in your bank account? That's okay, put it on a credit card. What if the money was gone? What if there was no money for gas or food? For hair color? Gone is the weekly housekeeper, the facials, shopping for a new outfit. The credit cards are maxed and your credit score is plummeting. Many of us go through life oblivious, believing that the money will always be there. Just like the looks that once gave us power. What if one day it was gone? What would you do?

I did not have a savings account. I did not have a

backup plan.

I came to California from Las Vegas to begin a career in real estate. I was hired to oversee a multi-million-dollar condominium project in Westwood. I oversaw the construction and then sold the condominiums, and managed the property.

When the real estate market crashed in the '80s, I moved away from real estate and returned to the legal profession as a legal assistant for a real estate attorney at one of the top law firms in LA. I needed a steady income.

Once the real estate market stabilized, I left the law office to begin my career in corporate real estate. For the next 25 years, this has been my passion.

In 1995, I started my own company, acting as the real estate department for many companies such as Penguin Yogurt, Marvelous Muffins, Blue Chip Cookies, Coffee Bean & Tea Leaf, Supercuts, and RadioShack.

I found my clients new locations all across southern California, managed their assets, renewed leases, lowered rents, and generally oversaw all aspects of their real estate and increased value.

In 2001, I met an amazing family who had come to Glendale from South America, and my client was primarily in the apartment business. He owned three retail centers at the time. One of these was a Target center located in Oceanside, California. One of my first projects was to sell this asset because Mr. B was getting older and did not want to drive so far to manage it every week. We sold that center and purchased the Plaza del Sol shopping center in Burbank. We went on to buy the Huntington Beach Plaza in Huntington Beach and the Garden Grove Shopping Center. I sold six of his projects in 2012: Garden Grove, Cypress, Huntington Beach, Redondo Beach, Cerritos, and Hawthorne Plaza.

I was privileged to know and work with Mr. B, and he affected me in a very positive way. He was always "Mr. B" to me. I never wanted to call him by his given name because he is the only man I respected enough to want to call "Mr." He was the most amazing person inside and out. He was brilliant, yet humble and approachable.

Mr. B was the father I would have wanted if I could have picked my own. He always showed me respect. He never criticized me, always encouraged me, and always saw me in the best light. He made me want to do my best and I wanted to honor him. I loved, respected and admired him.

I often wonder where I'd be if I'd had him to mold and guide my life. I never saw him angry—and was impressed at the way he gave the credit for his success to God. He consistently walked the walk and he modeled how to be in the world and love God.

He made a lasting impression on my life and I will never forget him.

His memory will live on in my heart and I will use it to honor him by being my best self and staying close to God. He is truly missed.

THIS AIN'T MY FIRST RODEO … or … DESPERATE TIMES CALL FOR DESPERATE ACTION.

Shortly after our marriage, husband number three and I started flipping houses, and we were good at it. The money started to roll in and just before the financial crash in 2008, we bought a restaurant. I'd made some large commissions on the shopping centers and it had always been my dream to own a pizza chain. I wanted to be the next Domino's!

I began looking at restaurants to buy and found one in our neighborhood. We plunked down $100,000 cash and bought the restaurant. I had gone to cooking school in Italy and was excited to come home and implement some of the recipes I learned there. It was a hard business and my husband and I had a lot to learn. There were days when the cook did not show up and we had to jump in and improvise. It was very stressful and the business did not give us the return we had hoped for. If we'd had a liquor license, it would have produced more income, but the city would have required an entire remodel for that and we did not have the capital or the resources.

My husband was working at our restaurant every day, but there was very little left after buying the food and paying the employees, and we were not able to cover the expenses. It was a stressful time.

Our flipping business came to a halt with the crash in

2008. Just as we could not take credit for the good fortune we had coming up, we could not take all of the blame for the real estate market crashing on the way down. It came fast and we were unaware and unprepared.

Like so many others, we lost our dream home, but luckily came out with enough cash after negotiating a short sale to get a small apartment for ourselves, two dogs, and a cat. It was cozy. After a year of living in that small one-bedroom apartment, my husband and I moved to a house we rented where we could give the horses, cat, and dogs room to run and enjoy the rural life. I worked my real estate business from home and my husband looked for a job. We decided to sell the restaurant. It had become too much work with too little reward. It was no longer worth the stress and was a strain on our relationship.

Unfortunately, we sold the restaurant at a loss.

Sadly, just like the restaurant, we could not heal our relationship. The pressures of the business and our poor communication style took their toll. We ended our 16-year marriage.

After we divorced, I made a large commission on a shopping center sale and was able to buy the house we'd been renting, reducing the monthly expense by $1,000 compared to what my husband and I were paying when we rented.

Two years later, I put $50,000 into remodeling the house and put it up for sale. Unfortunately, the market was depressed, and I was not able to make a profit on this house. If I knew then what I know now, I would have tried to make a deal with the lender and held on. But, once again, I needed the money. I was strapped for cash. Cash poor. That is often my story. Easy come and easy go. Fast in and fast out. I guess my Vegas days were still with me.

The pandemic caught everyone by surprise. No one saw it coming. Like the S&L crash of 2008, I was left holding the bag. I'm very grateful that I sold my spec property in January 2020, two months before the shit hit the fan. This was just a gift from God. But, I remember in 2008, when I was not so lucky. I had a good couple of years selling shopping centers and had been regularly flipping the houses I lived in. I was currently living in a home that I'd purchased for $1.2 million. I was already in the process of remodeling it when I became aware of the housing market coming to a screeching halt. Banks were foreclosing on loans and the real estate market crashed for all intents and purposes. I was struggling to make my payments.

* * * * *

A few years earlier, my mother had decided to retire and move to a senior retirement community in the high desert. Looking back, this was a crazy idea because she was only 55 and had no money saved for retirement. She asked me to buy the house she was leaving so that she could purchase the new one. Of course, the price she wanted was higher than the market value. I told her that I would make no money at that price. She didn't care. She told me that if I didn't follow through with the sale, she'd lose the deposit she put on the new house in Apple Valley and she'd be very unhappy.

So, I did what I thought a good daughter would do and bought the house at a premium. My mom moved into her dream home in the beautiful Del Webb retirement community, and I began construction on her old home with the intent to flip it. I remodeled the house and made it adorable. However, it did not bring the price I needed to make a profit, so I held on to it and rented it. I got one bad renter after another. After evicting the latest tenant and holding a worthless judgment, I did not know what I was going to do to keep the house. Looking back, I see many instances in my life where I took risks and exposed myself to financial vulnerability due to people-pleasing.

After some time, I rented the house to a man who paid rent for a few months and then stopped. I had to evict him. It was draining me to keep up with the mortgage payments on an empty house.

It was 2005 and pot shops were very popular. My stepson came to me and said he knew a guy who would rent the house for $5,000 per month in cash. I accepted right away, without too much thought. This income would cover the mortgage and give me a nice income. I knew he intended to use it as a grow house and I didn't care. This seemed like an answer to my dreams, but I remember being so nervous lying in my bed at night praying that nothing would go wrong. And of course, before long, it did. I got a call in the middle of the night from my stepson telling me the house had been raided and the cannabis confiscated. There were so many things wrong with this situation.

A. I'd not told my husband.
B. It was my mother's former neighborhood, so those people knew her, and it was embarrassing for her when the house got raided.
C. I lost revenue.
D. When the tenant got arrested and the pot operation shut down, they stopped paying rent. There was a lot of damage done to the house which had to be corrected, and it was costly.

As the income stopped coming in on this rental house, my real estate business flatlined and we were unable to make the payments on our primary residence.

It was a full-time job attempting to do a loan modification with the bank, preparing and sending, and then re-sending all required paperwork.

The tension between my husband and I was high. He did not agree with how fast we'd expanded and now felt worried and pressured, and he blamed me for putting us in this situation. My husband had lived a very frugal lifestyle up to this point.

We filed for bankruptcy. It was a tough time emotionally and financially for us. We fought a lot. My husband's mother died. He did not feel that I supported him. I felt he didn't save me. We were broken. We had ridden the roller coaster to the top and had been feeling so good, and now we were on the other side, plummeting down and screaming for our lives. We did not know what to do. My husband needed a hip replacement and I needed to work at the restaurant while he recovered. I was exhausted. I resented him. I was angry. I was afraid.

We were living above our means. We did not have any money saved. We did not budget. We would have done better to set aside some cash to have a safety net. I was impulsive and just went forward and hoped for the best.

YOU MAKE YOUR MONEY WHEN YOU BUY, NOT SELL

I was the broker on a property in Texas. It had a closed Burger King and Church's Chicken. I was representing the seller and I brought a buyer, so I controlled both sides. The buyer decided to drop out when he learned that there were underground environmental issues. My experience told me this was still a good site. I offered my client, the seller, a ridiculously low price of $125,000, and he accepted it. I was in shock but elated at the same time.

Now, the problem was coming up with the money. I had $30,000, not $125,000, to invest. After making a list of potential investors and calling everyone I could think of, I heard "NO" after "NO."

Finally, to my surprise, when telling a friend that I

needed the money for this deal, I was shocked to hear, "I will do this with you. Sign me up!"

"You're kidding?" I responded incredulously. I had no idea that this friend had this kind of money. She lived a very frugal lifestyle and, I learned that she had been looking for an investment herself.

I was able to subdivide the lot and sell one-half of the property for $350,000, and then sell the remaining parcel for $350,000, tripling our money. My intuition told me that this was a good project, and having purchased it so low, there was very little risk of the project failing. I was so grateful for this windfall (and so was my investor!).

ANOTHER CRASH

It took a global pandemic to wake me up. My eyes are now wide open. I see the corruption and how the government attempts to instill fear in people and control us through the media. The sheep mentality is in full effect. But for me, when the world stopped, I was blithely going through life with my blinders on, thinking I still had plenty of time to "get it together," make my mark, with nothing to worry about…and then, on March 18, 2020, the world as we know it changed. State officials told us to shelter in place and businesses were closing everywhere. My livelihood, commercial real estate, died. When this happened, I had no fallback plan. I had no savings. I had no income. I had one listing, but it was a "C" location, and non-essential retailers were not allowed to have businesses open, so my well of buyers immediately dried up.

In addition to the world ending, I was turning 65. This limited my ability to attract that knight in shining armor. I finally understood that I did not have a fairy godmother. I would have to save myself. In other words, if it was to be, it was up to me. This was a very scary realization.

With all of the newfound time I had to myself, I decided to take stock. This was a shocking and scary undertaking. I spent much more money than I made each month. I had no signs of future work coming and I was not getting any younger. My boat was sinking fast and I had only a thimble to bail the water out.

COVID was a scary time. I was lonely. I was anxious. I kept trying to fill the hole. No matter how much men, money, or food I used to distract the emptiness, it was never full. I was alone, I was full of pain. *Cry, cry, cry, eat, eat, eat, spend, spend, spend...howl at the moon.* I felt like a feral wolf inside, howling in despair.

Will I ever make money again? I asked myself. *What am I here for? What am I good at? How do I get out of here and find a place I can afford to be? Will I be okay?* These are the questions that ran through my mind at 3 am, as I stared at the ceiling.

* * * * *

We need to assess our situation and see where we are. Only then can we move forward and see where we are going. To weather the real estate crash, I tried to move forward by starting a short-term rental business. It was successful and I grew the portfolio to six AirBnB units. It worked and I did my best. I was happy that I could help people by providing them with work. I employed cleaners and handymen who lived near my units. My goal was to get solvent.

My mission was to love my life and afford it. I wanted to continue to grow my real estate company and make it my best year yet. That meant I had to reach $800k in income. I began to have faith that the universe would provide my wildest dreams.

But no matter how much money I made, it was gone within a couple of years and the feeling of being broke returned. The cycle kept repeating.

I continued to ask myself, what is my life about now? Why do I find myself cash-poor? What is the lesson I need to learn?

I began to go within and listen to God. Each morning I would meditate and ask for guidance.

The answer that came was to be cautious, resourceful, and have a plan B. It was time to prune. Time for new growth. Slow down and go within. Go back to basics.

I needed to pare down my life, even though I didn't know where or how to begin.

You can live on less, I heard the voice inside my head say. *You don't have to trade time for money. Trust me. Trust the unlimitedness of the universe.*

I reduced my overhead and stopped spending money I didn't have. I began to wash my dogs in the shower with me. That felt good. I washed the sheets. That felt good. I did the dishes. That felt good. I began to keep my bedroom tidy—now I will attack the paper piles in my office. Esteemable acts build self-esteem.

That day I decided. I will get my joy back. I will exude joy and abundance and compassion and serenity. I will smile and I will spread love. I am here to love. Be love. Give love. Accept love. I'm worth it. All is well.

* * * * *

When COVID-19 hit, I was recently divorced, and I had had a few years living off the settlement from the sale of my house. Life was pretty good. I thought I was just waiting for my next relationship. I did not know then what I came to know. If you want to hear God laugh, tell him your plans.

My money had dwindled and my business had evaporated. The consulting work I was doing was two hours away, and COVID had shut down my client's office. I needed to size down and get my overhead down quickly. My plan was to move somewhere I could afford and still have room for my animals.

Have you ever noticed how many times we've bought something or spent money on something to assuage our emotions? What would you do if suddenly it was not there? It just was not there. It is a terrible feeling. One day, I realized I did not have the means to buy a gift for a friend's wedding, a gift for my new grandchild's birthday. In fact, I did not have money to buy dog food. I was completely out of money. Then, I looked around to see what I had. Things that I thought had value didn't. I put them on Craigslist, eBay, Offer Up, and FB Marketplace. Everyone else was out of money, too.

What do we do when we don't have enough money for the basic necessities? This particular time I was saved by friends. One bought my beloved Louis Vuitton bag that I had bought in Paris and another bought home furnishings that she had admired and which I no longer needed. The things I had collected, hoarded, or coveted no longer had meaning for me. They had served their purpose and I was ready to let them go.

Going through this financial crunch has caused me to see through a different lens. I used to see people asking for money and would hand them a dollar but not think much more about their plight. Now, they were my peers. I was just like them, living social security check to social security check, and it did not go far enough. I was underwater. I did not make enough to cover my basic monthly needs.

I decided to make a change!

Mourning my old life was difficult. The lunches in Beverly Hills, the trips to the spa, the front row seats at concerts, private jet travel, yacht parties, and the like. All distant memories now. Those things were fun. But I had become numb to them and didn't appreciate them at the time. Only when they were gone could I see how good things had been. Contrast is a great teacher.

There are days now when I'm not sure how I'll come up with $35 for a bale of hay to feed my horses. This is light-years away from where I was then.

If we can get completely present in the NOW and appreciate and thank God for what we have, we will know joy.

Learn to accept what is, find the humility to appreciate and be grateful for what you do have, and realize that all you need is being provided for you today. Just today.

If we stay in *this* day and use our minds to solve the needs we have right now, we can let go of stress for the unknown of tomorrow. When tomorrow becomes today, we will have what we need to solve those problems. We can trust God to know this. He has us in the palm of his hand.

God, you said, I would lend and not borrow. Send me money to pay all of my bills and return the money to those who have loaned me so that I can better serve you and do your work. There are so many people who I want to help, who have helped me. I want to be an example of what is possible.

* * * * *

One day, I was at the market getting some things for my next few meals. The bill was $75.32. It seemed like I could not go into the store anymore for less than $80.00. This was the universe's cruel joke. I handed the clerk my card.

"Denied," she said.

"What?" I croaked. "That's not possible." I was sure I'd checked my balance before I left the house.

"Do you have another card?" the checker asked. I fumbled in my purse and handed her my business debit card.

"Denied," she reported in an even tone. I was mortified. I was embarrassed, frustrated, and hungry. There was a line of five people. I turned to look apologetically at the woman behind me. She was tattooed on both arms, had a pierced nose, and a mohawk.

"I've got you," she said.

"I only have $35 cash," I said to the clerk, mortified. "Let's remove items until we get down to $35."

The woman in line said to her, "Keep it all and put it all on my tab."

I looked at her and said, "I can't let you do that."

At that point, the guy behind her poked his head out and said kindly, "Hey, we've all been there, believe me! I'd like to pay for it, too."

As I was counting out my $35 in cash to the clerk, I realized I was still short $2, and, noticing this, the bag boy stopped bagging and reached into his pocket, pulled out his wallet, and handed me $5.

"Thank you," I said, with tears streaming down my face, completely humbled. What a show of support and love, from strangers. I was totally supported on that day. That had never happened to me in my 60 years on the planet in so-called high-income demographic areas. The people here in this town of 900 care for each other.

Like the neighbor who loaned me a solar trailer to run my lights. Like my other neighbor who had a port-a-potty delivered. Like the neighbor who sent kiddie swimming pools for my dogs and brought hoses so I wouldn't have to walk to the well several times per day to carry water to my horses. God sent so many angels to me during this time. It felt like I was meant to be here.

Once we finally got the well to work and got the water working in the house, the temperature was beginning to drop. It was getting cold and I had no heating. I had run out of money AGAIN. I went to the local hardware store where I had been buying all of my supplies. I found the owner, Herb, whom I had gotten to know over the past months, and asked him if he would sell me a hot water heater and let me pay him when I could. "Yes," he said. God is truly good.

Next, I needed to fundraise. I began to look around my house for things that might have value. I had items that were 50 years old. I opened an eBay account and posted these items there. There is a Google app that, if you don't know the value of an item, you take a picture of it and it will tell you the history and value of the item. You can also see on eBay what others are selling items for. Next, I learned that if you find artwork at a flea market or garage sale that is painted on canvas with a signature and number on it, chances are it is valuable. Put that on eBay. Google the artist's name and find out what their other artwork goes for.

One day, low on funds, I did an inventory and realized that I still had the St. Louis crystal glasses and 12-piece Christofle sterling flatware from my marriage 30 years ago. It was an asset and time to sell. I placed it with the local auction house and waited for news they had sold. The buyer that I sold them to was an avid entertainer and she was thrilled. I put $1,000 in my pocket—it was a win-win!

You can sell your assets and put an ad on Craigslist for your services. Sell what you can and reduce your expenses.

There is also an app called REAL REAL. The rep comes to your house and looks at your designer clothing, jewelry, and sunglasses. Then they bag and list each item and put it on their website. Soon, it sells and you get a check.

Have a yard sale. Apps like Offer Up and Facebook Marketplace work great.

Start a business. I was low on funds and looking for a side hustle when I saw a webinar about AirBnB. I paid for the course. I followed the instructions and I found an apartment in Newport Beach and furnished it with furniture from Goodwill and my own home. Then I posted a profile and turned it on. Soon, I heard the ding on my phone notifying me that I'd made my first reservation. It was so exciting. For a year, this was a very fun and lucrative venture, until the pandemic hit.

You can rent out one of the rooms in your house to a traveling nurse or college student.

Use your property as a film site. If your property is not conducive to that, be an agent for someone who is. Several years back, Walmart used my property for a Thanksgiving commercial that aired during the Super Bowl. It was lucrative and I was very proud to see it on TV.

Take in a dog for doggie daycare.

Reduce expenses: Cut out all monthly subscription fees. Let go of Direct TV or cable TV. Get a smart TV and a streaming channel to watch your news.

Be an UBER driver. Deliver UberEats.

Use your talents and turn it into a business.

Offer to tutor children whose parents can't handle homeschooling.

House sit.

Become a translator.

Another way to create funds is to manifest it. Several times a day visualize money pouring into your bank account.

We can look to the Bible for all of God's promises. If we believe, we can recite these promises daily and often. God, you said: You plan to prosper us (Jeremiah 29:11), so Lord, cause me to prosper according to your word. Thank you for the people that you have assigned to bless my life financially. Bless them even more abundantly for their obedience. In God's name, amen.

This is where an affirmation comes into play. Plug your name into the following affirmation. "I, Deborah, receive vast amounts of money from various sources on a continuous basis." Say this over and over, adding, "I, Deborah, am a magnet for money." "I, Deborah, make money easily." Write these down, post them on your computer monitor, and repeat them out loud several times per day. Next, take action.

Make a generous donation to something or someone. *This works*. Pick someone anonymously who could use the help and mail money to them. Buy food for the person in the car behind you at the drive-through. Pay for someone's meal at a restaurant. These gestures tell the universe that you are a giver and money will come back to you.

Money is energy and there is plenty of it for you and everyone else. That is why it is called currency. Think of it like a bolt of electricity. Do not stress about money. Slow down and be grateful for where you are in life. Focus on what you do have and not what you don't have. When you are grateful for what you have, you will receive more of it. Vibrate and align yourself with gratitude and continually affirm, "I have all that I need."

There will be setbacks. Let go of perfection. Keep your focus on what you are striving for and keep reaching toward your goal without punishing yourself. Let go of the outcome. Do your best. Take the next right action. Think progress, not perfection. That's enough.

I HAVE ENOUGH, I DO ENOUGH, I AM ENOUGH. YOU ARE ENOUGH.

ALL IS WELL. I WILL FIND MY JOY TODAY.
ALL IS WELL AND LIFE IS GOOD.

CHAPTER 10

Cross Addictions

Just when I thought that my self-sabotaging obsession had ended, I noticed that I was acting out again. Why did I keep scrolling on Amazon? Why could I not stop binge-watching a Netflix series? Why did my meal feel like it was "not enough?"

I have not used drugs since the '80s. I haven't had alcohol since 2011, and I've had multiple years of no flour or sugar. I am in a healthy-sized body. But with no man to fill that empty hole inside, I still feel the rumblings of discontent. Fear, doubt, and insecurity. I still want to feel validated by having a man love me. Cherish me. Not having a relationship makes me want to eat, shop, or do anything that will fill this dark, empty hole.

This was cross-addiction. In my food program, we say, "Thin is not well." Because, unless we look at what is underneath the eating, drinking, shopping, or sleeping around, we will continue to use.

The addiction or inability to stop the behavior of the addiction is just a symptom of the trauma or pain-body, a concept introduced by Echkhart Tolle in his book, *A New Earth*. The pain-body can manifest in many ways including anger, self-hate, anxiety, and depression.

I needed to be brave and go deeper. I needed to shine the light on the trauma of my childhood so that I could understand it and heal it.

Many, if not most of us, have several of these addictions or band-aids that we use to cope. Whether it is medicating with drugs and/or alcohol, an action such as overeating, or sexual or love addiction, we notice we have adopted a crutch. This became true for me early on.

A lonely, only child, I needed validation and attention from a father figure who was not able to give it. The situation was formed early on and when this proved frustrating, I used food and then drugs to ease the pain. My problem was low self-esteem and it caused many destructive situations in my life. It caused me to make bad choices. I never felt good enough. I still struggle with it occasionally today. Even after losing 75 pounds, keeping it off for years, and having made a high six-figure income for the past four years, I still continually have to fight the feeling that everyone is better than me.

It is painful and difficult. Intellectually, I know that I'm worthy. My spiritual connection tells me that I'm good enough, that I do enough and have enough. I remind myself daily to breathe, believe, and give thanks to God for the great abundance that he has showered on me. I find that I have to take this in and lead with my intention. My intention is to show up and do God's work, give service and reach out to others. To be my best self and just give love. Living in the present and vibrating at a higher level. Leaving the outcome to God. Letting him work through me and letting my inner light shine.

Addiction is when we continue doing something destructive even when we don't want to continue doing it. Another way to see if we are addicted is to notice if we can't stop once we start. I'm addicted to buttered popcorn. Not at a movie theater. Only my own. Made by me at home and consumed alone. I eat in a ritualistic fashion. I have my favorite things that I have to prepare a certain way and consume in front of the TV alone. I'd never eat this way if someone was present.

At a recent business lunch, I ordered a healthy salad. The food was delicious, but I was not focused on it. I was excited about the business I was discussing with the prospect. The food I eat alone at home is the hit. The hit to calm me down and soothe me. To help me check out or zone out. Addictive eating for me is also about trying to get as much in as I can. I'm trying to fill that hole of nervousness, worry, loneliness, whatever feeling is trying to come up.

Often, we put down one addiction and then discover that we have picked up another. This is called transferring obsessions. We can have many and multiple addictions. It's what happens when we try to fill the hole within.

For those of us who have childhood trauma, we have ways of coping, whether it is drugs, alcohol, food, sex, or shopping. These things help us dull the pain when the feelings become too intense.

I was so unequipped to deal with my emotions and the pain of my childhood that I needed to medicate anytime a feeling came up.

I now know that it isn't a weakness, it is just our chosen coping mechanism to help us get by when the pain from the past comes up. I used food for years to dull the pain of my emptiness. I tried drugs, I tried alcohol, I tried food, and I tried all three together, but I could never get numb enough.

We can spend our entire lives running from our past experiences, but they never truly leave us. This is an ongoing process. A work in progress.

The truth is, it's a lifelong journey. I know this to be true because I still sometimes struggle with how to cope with a feeling.

We can retrain our minds. Practice letting your thoughts go through your mind. Don't judge them. Just notice them. The idea is to get them up and out, and over much time and practice, we can identify and revisit the pain we felt and then try to go inside and heal it. We can do this with meditation.

By becoming aware of our thoughts, we can then listen to what we believe about the situation and listen to our thoughts around it. We do this by looking at how these negative thoughts are creating negative feelings and impacting our actions which hold us back in life. Once we change these thoughts, we can explore different actions and have different outcomes.

Once I realized that my affliction was the result of my choices and not a disease, I began to take back control. I could control myself if I slowed down and acted in a way that my future self would, like not eating flour or sugar. I just don't eat it. Not because I'm weak, but because I have recognized it isn't good for me and I love myself enough to not want that in my body. Also, I recognize that one bite of flour or sugar starts up an uncontrollable craving, that if I act on it, I can't stop, so I just don't start. This is not a moral issue. It is just a fact. It is what it is.

The same with men. I can feel completely myself, and at ease, and then once I begin to engage in behavior with a man, such as texting or having uncommitted sex, it sets up a craving. I'm then thrown into a spiral of obsession and self-doubt that leaves me spinning. I used to say "My picker is broken," but now I say, "I love myself so much that I will only spend time with quality men who are worthy of me."

This is also true with money. I recognize that I have a tendency to overspend, so I slow down and ask myself what will serve my goals and what I'm trying to accomplish.

I have found a way to manage these cross-addictions by not reacting to the emotions behind the feelings. Instead, if I slow down before taking the addictive action and ask myself what would serve the person that I am meant to be because I love and approve of myself, I choose the correct path and take the next right action. Also, when a craving comes up, I can take a PAUSE. The acronym is "Pause Action Until Serenity Returns." By doing this exercise every day, I can achieve my goals and feel at peace. Esteemable acts bring self-esteem.

A person with an addictive personality can do anything to excess and call it an addiction. It can be gum, Diet Coke, or Splenda. It can be texting, video games, or binge-watching Netflix. Whatever we are using is a mechanism to take us away from ourselves. Our feelings. Our fears. It is either our saboteur or our savior. We get to choose. The important thing is that we give it time and attention. These thoughts are creating our feelings and need to be looked at. Only when we shine the light on our thoughts will we heal our past trauma and beliefs. Once we identify them, we can heal them and move forward.

Is addiction a choice or a disease?

For years, I resisted joining a 12-step program because I did not want to say that I had a disease. I felt it was a choice. I thought that if I only had more willpower, I could overcome it on my own.

The nature of addiction is a complex and widely debated topic. Different perspectives exist regarding whether addiction is primarily a choice or a disease.

When I Googled, I saw many conflicting opinions.

One perspective argues that addiction is the result of

individual choices and behaviors. It suggests that people willingly engage in substance use or addictive behaviors and continue to do so despite the negative consequences. According to this viewpoint, addiction is seen as a series of choices made by the individual, and overcoming addiction requires personal responsibility and willpower.

Another perspective, supported by medical and scientific research, considers addiction as a chronic, relapsing brain disease. This viewpoint emphasizes that addiction involves changes in the brain's structure and function, impacting decision-making, impulse control, and reward mechanisms. Addiction is believed to result from a combination of genetic, environmental, and biological factors. Advocates of the disease model argue that addiction is not merely a matter of personal choice but rather a complex condition requiring medical treatment, behavioral interventions, and support.

Some experts propose an integrated perspective that combines elements of choice and disease models. This viewpoint acknowledges that initial substance use or behavior may involve voluntary choices, but over time, addiction can alter brain chemistry and impair an individual's ability to exert full control over their behavior. It recognizes the role of personal agency and responsibility while acknowledging the biological and psychological aspects of addiction.

What I have found after years of research is that, for me, I can control my compulsion *until* I take the first bite.

Once I take the first bite, the first drink, send the first text, or swipe the credit card, it is game over. I can't stop. It was then that I realized that my addiction causes me to feel dis-ease. So, although not a medical condition that needed treatment, it was an emotional feeling of discomfort in my body.

Ultimately, understanding addiction as a complex interplay between choice and disease can help shape effective interventions and policies that address both the personal responsibility of individuals and the underlying physiological and psychological factors contributing to addiction.

It became clear to me that my addiction played out in different forms. Just when I thought I had my food under control, I noticed that I wanted to shop. If I curtailed the spending, I wanted to eat. I needed to go online and scroll for hours on Amazon, eBay, or Craigslist. Or, if I watched a Netflix program, I was binge-watching it and needed to continue until the entire series was done. If a man showed any interest, I was fantasizing about marrying him and the mental obsession began.

After my marriage to Tom ended, the subsequent breakup with Eli, and the social annihilation by people knowing that I had the affair, I was lost. My world was upside down with pain and longing, but slowly I pulled myself together and buried myself in my work.

When my employer let me know that they were eliminating my job in California, I was devastated. They said I could keep my job only if I moved to the corporate headquarters in Texas. Leaving my family, sunny California, and the ocean was not an option for me, so I gave my notice. I asked my former boss whether if I went out on my own, I could keep them as a client, and to my delight, he said yes.

So, I hunkered down and began to study for the broker's exam. Every day I ate and studied, and I ate some more. Months later, I took the exam, became a broker, and opened my own office. The day I passed the broker's exam was such a happy one. I was very proud of myself, but my weight had once again ballooned up. I had lived alone in a small bungalow in Santa Monica for five years and I was single. I dated occasionally, but the guys were not a fit. Maybe I was too fat. This was, after all, Los Angeles, and there was a lot of competition. The guys would say, "Pretty face, but ..." After a while, I came to see that I unconsciously kept the weight on to keep the men away. I had not resolved my past issues with men and love. I needed to stay safe.

The phenomenon of cross-addictions, also known as addiction transfer or addiction substitution, refers to the occurrence of an individual replacing one addictive behavior or substance with another. It involves shifting from one form of addiction to another, often due to underlying psychological or physiological factors.

Cross-addictions can manifest in different ways, such as switching from one substance to another (e.g., substituting alcohol addiction with drug addiction), transitioning from a substance addiction to a behavioral addiction (e.g., replacing drug addiction with gambling or compulsive shopping), or even transferring from one behavior addiction to another (e.g., replacing gambling addiction with food addiction).

Several factors contribute to the development of cross-addictions:

- **Underlying Vulnerabilities:** Individuals with addictive tendencies may have underlying vulnerabilities that make them more prone to addictive behaviors. These vulnerabilities can include genetic factors, co-occurring mental health conditions, trauma, or a history of substance abuse.

- **Common Underlying Mechanisms:** Various addictive substances and behaviors can activate similar brain pathways involved in reward, pleasure, and reinforcement. This shared neurobiological basis can make individuals susceptible to developing new addictions as they seek alternative sources of gratification.

- **Unresolved Issues and Coping Strategies:** Addiction often stems from attempts to cope with underlying emotional or psychological issues. If these issues remain unresolved, individuals may turn to new addictive behaviors or substances as a way to continue self-medicating and avoiding the root causes of their addiction.

- **Replacement Behaviors:** When individuals eliminate or reduce one addictive behavior, they may seek alternative ways to fill the void left by the initial addiction. Without addressing the underlying motivations and developing healthier coping strategies, individuals may transition to new addictive patterns.

Addressing cross-addictions requires a comprehensive approach that includes:

- **Identifying Underlying Issues:** It is crucial to identify and address the underlying emotional, psychological, or traumatic factors contributing to addictive behaviors. This may involve therapy, counseling, or support groups to develop healthier coping mechanisms.

- **Comprehensive Treatment:** Seeking professional help through addiction specialists, therapists, or medical professionals can provide support in managing cross-addictions. Customized treatment plans that address both the specific addiction and the underlying factors are important.

- **Support Networks:** Engaging with support groups, such as 12-step programs or counseling, can provide valuable peer support and guidance throughout the recovery process.

- **Lifestyle Changes:** Adopting healthy lifestyle choices, such as regular exercise, stress management techniques, balanced nutrition, and pursuing meaningful activities, can help break the cycle of addiction and replace it with positive habits.

Understanding the phenomenon of cross-addictions highlights the importance of holistic approaches to addiction treatment, addressing underlying issues, and developing healthier coping strategies to promote long-term recovery and well-being.

I've found that for me, the most effective course of action that helped me heal my childhood trauma and manage my addiction is through the study of the 12 steps of Alcoholics Anonymous.

CHAPTER 11

Five Hours with Wayne Dyer

O ur vacation was over and we were headed back to reality. My third husband and I had just spent five days on Maui. Our relationship had cooled down and something was definitely missing, but we had nonetheless enjoyed ourselves.

"Did you have fun, honey?" James asked as we sat in our UBER headed to the airport to catch our flight home.

"I loved it!" I answered, a half truth. We had been at a beautiful resort in a magical place, but the romance I'd hoped for was lacking. My weight was over 200 pounds, and I felt like a beached whale. I think that James was disappointed that the cute, size-six girl he'd married had vanished and an angry, size-16 woman had replaced her. He was right. I was angry. I was disappointed. On top of it all I was ashamed of how I looked.

The stress was catching up to me. I was working as hard as I could and I could not seem to get anywhere. I felt like a rat on a wheel. Round and round I would go and always, I would remain in the same place. That is, if I managed not to fall off the wheel altogether.

We had married. We had bought a home. James began to work long hours and traveled a lot. I was alone and I was packing on the weight. I had heavy issues and it showed. I had become pregnant but lost the baby. It was devastating to me because that was why I had gotten married—years earlier, I had chosen to terminate an early pregnancy, and now I felt it was my time to have a baby and wanted James to be the father of my children. He had two beautiful boys and I knew that our children would be beautiful. But it was not meant to be. I had a miscarriage and subsequently found out that James was cheating on me. Many events knocked the bloom off the rose, but it seemed that I was punishing myself for all of them. I felt unlovable. Our sex life had vanished.

I began to resent and blame him. My life was half over, and what did I have to show for it? An absent, cheating husband, angry stepchildren, and a body that was unrecognizable to me.

As we settled into our first-class seats in the middle aisle, a man put his small bag in the overhead bin and began to slide in next to me. I looked up and my mouth fell open. It was the amazing Wayne Dyer. He was tan and fit and had the iconic cap on his head. I was sitting next to a man that I had idolized for years. I had all of his books and tapes and I greatly admired his wisdom and humble attitude.

He looked over at me, smiled, held out his hand, and simply said,

"Hi, I'm Wayne."

As we chatted amicably, he told me about his home on Maui and his children, and as we waited for the flight attendant to bring our food, I told him my story. With my husband sleeping in the window seat, I explained how I struggled with my weight and how my marriage was suffering.

He listened. He was so warm and so encouraging. He talked about how addiction had affected him and how his family still struggled with it. His cell phone rang and he took a call from one of his children.

"Skylar," I heard him ask, "did you go to your meeting?" I couldn't help but overhear and smile to myself. This guy knew what I was talking about. He walked the talk.

We chatted the entire flight, and as we began our descent, he pulled out a book and a Sharpie and began to write in it.

"You know, Deborah," he said, "you can turn this all around beginning now. Just believe it and think it is possible and it will come to pass." He handed me his book titled *10 Secrets for Success and Inner Peace*, which he had inscribed with "To Deborah ~ all things are possible if we just believe. Love, Wayne."

This book spoke of having an open mind full of possibilities. All possibilities. Dr. Dyer cautioned against getting pigeonholed into one concept or modality. Many roads lead to Rome. He recommends staying open to everything and attached to nothing. This mindset promotes peace and equanimity. Turn the process over to God or your higher power. Let them work out the "how." Keep your focus on the result and how you will feel when you have your desired object or outcome.

This time spent with one of my heroes changed my life. It's one of those serendipitous moments they speak about in the Celestine Prophecy. We must pay attention to who we meet and listen for guidance. The universe is sending us signs and messages all the time to help us. I went home after that meeting and I changed my life. I recommitted to having no flour, sugar, or alcohol, and I've been doing that now for more than a decade.

Dr. Dyer imparted so much wisdom during our flight together, but one message stood out, and that is the message of gratitude and humility. If we look at everything with grateful eyes, our hearts will soften. We are not owed anything. Anything we get is a gift. We aren't promised a job, a long life, good health, or a loving relationship. If we have it, it is purely a gift imparted from God or the universe and we have to view it as such.

Lose the sense of entitlement and so many of our

problems will go away. Live humbly and appreciate everything that we have, good or bad. If it is less than what we want, we can view it as a lesson or a challenge—something that God has put in front of us to strengthen us.

Wayne Dyer continues to impact my life today. His study and explanation of the Tao Te Ching showed me that we need to be humble. Let go of entitlement. If we woke up today, that was a gift, not a given. The world owes us nothing, so anything and everything that we obtain are things to be celebrated and appreciated. We must exude gratitude to our higher power for these gifts. They were given to us. Dr. Dyer's memoir, *I Can See Clearly Now,* details his journey and life's work. He is an amazing example of what can be done when we continue to put in the effort, keep a good attitude, and believe in the outcome.

After my chance encounter with Wayne Dyer, I began to meditate every day following the methods of the Tao, using the sound of God's name repeated over and over. Using this mantra gets us in touch with our higher power and helps us to realize that we are made in God's image. With God, all things are possible. We don't have to wish for something to happen in the future; we need only imagine that it has already happened. Play the video of what we wish for over and over again on the screen of our minds. It will come to pass. We must only stay in the present moment and act as if.

Let yourself feel the way you would feel if you already had what you'd wished for. Our mind takes this as a directive and makes it happen.

Dr. Dyer believes that he was chosen to shine the light on right living and living a life with integrity. He was one of my teachers and his books and teachings live on to guide us in living a positive and abundant life.

My friend Deb says that our lives are like a tapestry, which at the time I thought was very poetic and apropos, but upon closer reflection, I realize that my life is like a mosaic. It is a thing of beauty that has come as a result of lots of broken pieces and sharp edges coming together for the end product. Still beautiful, a scene that has come together by broken pieces being deliberately placed and held together with strong adhesive.

Dr. Dyer's core message was incredibly simple and equally profound: You are the same as your Source. You are God. Because you come from God, you cannot be anything but God. All of Dr. Dyer's work boils down to helping people realize this fundamental truth and overcome obstacles to living lives that fully recognize it.

In his book, *The Tao Te Ching*, Dr. Dyer teaches that we are all God. We are born in God's image. I AM means God. I AM is a pronouncement of who we are and the qualities we aspire to have. We are here to make our desires a reality. He instructs us to create a list of our I AMs.

LOOK AT THEM AND RECITE THEM <u>ALOUD</u>
THREE TIMES A DAY.

(Use my mantras until you find your own. Recite them over and over until they are ingrained in you and you believe them).

I AM ALIVE
I AM STRONG
I AM AFFLUENT
I AM WELL
I AM SATISFIED

My divorce from James had been final for about four months when I attended a writing workshop in San Francisco. This seminar was being put on by Hay House, the publishing company founded by the late Louise Hay, author of *You Can Heal Your Life*. The guest speaker was Wayne Dyer and I wanted to meet with him again. I wanted him to know how much he had inspired me on that plane ride back from Maui and how much his encouragement helped me get abstinent and healthy, and I wanted to thank him.

I was excited to be in the city of my birth and excited to take this workshop and learn how to get the story inside me onto paper. I had wanted to write for so long but it always took a back seat to the business of real life and making money to support myself. Dr. Dyer showed me that it is important to follow our dreams and that it is never too late. I'm so grateful to have met him and as a result, it is my life's work to pass along his teachings to others.

CHAPTER 12

For The Love of The Horse

The real estate market was booming. We sold our house in Woodland Hills at a very nice profit and began negotiating to make this new home ours. We agreed on the price and opened escrow. After a physical inspection, I informed the seller we needed to lower the purchase price based on all of the deferred maintenance work the house needed. I fancied myself quite the astute negotiator and was unprepared when the seller said, "Sorry, we can't lower the purchase price—but we'll throw in the horses."

…Throw in the horses??? What? I thought. To make a long story short, it seemed like the universe was conspiring to make my childhood dream come true. To own this beautiful house with horses, too? To my surprise, I heard myself say, "Sure," and the rest is history.

* * * * *

My third husband James and I had moved to the San Fernando Valley from Santa Monica in 1977, shortly after we married.

We were both working hard and slowly building our real estate portfolio. We were on our third house flip when we fell in love with a sprawling country estate in need of some TLC in an upscale rural community outside of Los Angeles.

Not long after settling into our new digs, I called the facility that was boarding my recently inherited horses. They were nearby at a neighbor's ranch. Later that week, I arranged to meet them. On the appointed day, I walked down, introduced myself, and asked if I could see the horses. I was armed with carrots and lots of excitement. I was awestruck when I saw them and I could not believe my luck. There in the stalls, happily munching hay, were two beautiful white horses that looked up inquisitively when I came closer.

"Hi babies," I said softly, reaching out my hand to them, revealing a bite-size piece of carrot. They cautiously moved closer, sniffed the treat, then gently took the morsel from my hand and began to chew.

These two beauties were stunning and had such a look of intelligence about them. I returned daily, armed with carrots and treats, to earn their trust and friendship.

Jeannie Wallace was a long-time equestrian and a very strong horsewoman in the community who was an advocate of horsekeeping and maintaining the trails all along the Santa Monica mountains. I felt fortunate to meet her and was so grateful that she took me under her wing and began to teach me about these horses and their history. The horses' breed was National Show Horse, which is a mix of half Arabian and half American Saddlebred. They were mother and daughter. Sparkle was the 12-year-old mother and Ditto was her six-year-old mare. Over the next months, I spent hours with them every day and began to learn their moods and personalities.

Although I rode as a child, it had been years, and the horses I rode then had all been very calm and used to strangers and novices riding them. One day after a successful trail ride on Sparkle, and seeing Jeannie ride Ditto, she made it look so easy that I said, "I'm ready," feeling brave.

"Okay, let's do it," Jeannie said.

I put my helmet on, jumped up, and took a spin around the arena. Like a scene out of rodeo, Ditto unexpectedly spooked to the left, and in a flash, I was hurled out of the saddle to the right and landed hard on the dirt with a thud. The wind was knocked out of me and I laid there for a moment wondering if I was alive. From that moment, and for some time afterward, I was afraid of the horses. This set me back. To build up my confidence again, I began joining every horse clinic I could and spent hours each day trying to build their trust and my confidence.

In the beginning, the horses and I went through several stables looking for the right accommodations. We went to Malibu and it was great, however, Chris, the trainer there, believed in building a relationship before riding. So, for four months, I just visited and watched her lunge them. I wanted to ride, not watch. I felt like Goldilocks and wondered when or whether I'd ever find the right fit. We moved to yet another facility, this one was bigger, but the problem was finding time in the arena that fit my schedule. I was still green and needed assistance saddling and tacking up the horse.

After all of the starts and stops, I finally moved them to my property, where I could look out any window from my beautiful home and see them grazing in the field beyond the garden. This brought me so much joy. They are now where they were meant to be.

"Are you ever gonna ride those horses?" Jeannie asked when stopping by one day, "Or just feed them carrots? They are getting fat!"

"Uh, yeah," I said, "Soon."

"You need to get in a class," Jeannie said. "Call Karen." She gave me a number scribbled on a piece of paper. This was before cell phones.

"Okay, thanks," I said.

Karen was a local Calabasas resident who owned the popular tack shop. She was an experienced rider and held classes at the nearby Agoura arena twice a week. She was sharp and didn't take crap from anyone.

"Hi, Karen, this is Deborah. Jeannie gave me your number—I'm new to town. I'm a new rider and want to come to class but I don't know how to get there."

"Do you have a truck?" she asked.

"Yes, and I have a trailer, but don't know how to drive it."

"Okay," she said. "Call Rick and tell him Karen said to help you."

I was open to getting to riding class, but I didn't know how I was going to get there. I'd never had a truck before and certainly did not know how to pull horses.

I called Rick and made an appointment for the following day.

Trailer lessons.

The next day I was out brushing my horse when a white F250 pulled into the drive and my jaw dropped as the best-looking cowboy I'd ever seen got out and started walking over to me. Picture a taller, slimmer Rip from Yellowstone.

"Hi, I'm Rick," he said, extending his hand. He had on 501 jeans with cowboy boots, a plain shirt, and a black cowboy hat. His green eyes sparkled and his slow smile expressed a knowledge and confidence that was very appealing.

"So, you want to learn to trailer, huh?" Rick said.

"Yes, I need to get to horse class and back."

"Okay, it's gonna take a little time. Let's see your rig," Rick said.

We settled on a price and I walked Rick over to my

Navy Blue F350 truck that I'd just purchased.

"Okay, " he said. "See that hitch?" He pointed to the back of my truck. "You're gonna back up until that little ball goes into the hitch on that trailer." He might have been speaking Greek for all I knew.

This was all new to me. I was a city girl and had never owned a truck or a trailer, for that matter. After many tries and misses, Rick got an idea. "Okay, where's your tool shed?"

Frustrated, I pointed to the garage. Rick returned with a roll of blue painter's tape. He tore off a piece and put it on the inside of the door on my truck bed above the hitch.

"Okay, get in," he said, and I did. "Can you see the tape from your rearview mirror?"

"Yes," I said.

"Okay, good. Use that blue tape to line up your truck with the trailer hitch."

"Uh, okay," I said, eyes glued to the rearview, and pulled forward to get the truck straight, located the tape, lined it up in front of the hitch, and slowly backed up. Miraculously, it lined up! I did it. I was thrilled. Next, the hard part of lifting the trailer so that I could slide the hitch under it. This took many tries. I was so close each time. But it required patience and I had to keep getting in and out of the truck. Finally, too many times to count later, it lined up and I heard the click as the hitch went over the ball, and boom—the truck was holding up the trailer! Success!

Now the fun part of getting my horse into the trailer!

"Great job," Rick said. "We'll save that for the day of class."

For the next year, Rick taught me how to load the horses, drive the trailer, and improve my groundwork and trail riding. Our work together taught me to be confident in taking my horses places on my own and riding them in new areas. I will always be grateful for Rick and his friendship. My time with him and our time spent together on the horses was like a Zen experience for me. Rick was a guide and a guru to me. His teachings changed my life. He helped me become independent and strong with the horses. He was patient, ethical, and kind. He was a family man and demonstrated the highest integrity. Sadly, a time came when Rick's day job took him out of town and, just like David Caine's character, Grasshopper, in the 1975 western TV series *Kung Fu*, I had to take the reins and grow on my own to my next chapter.

The previous owner of this property had meant to bring the horses here and enjoy them, but tragically, his wife died and he could not bear to stay there or to spend time with them. It is very gratifying to me that the horses and I have found each other, and I can truly say that we have bonded. I thought I was rescuing them, but as it turns out, they were rescuing me. They captured my heart. My favorite time of day is 6:30 am, when I am feeding them and mucking their stalls as I listen to them happily eating. I spent the next year learning to ride my horses and discovering some of the trails near my home in Calabasas.

For me, the hardest part of boarding horses on my property was tearing myself away to work. Between conference calls, you could find me down at the barn with my girls!

This truly was the best time of my life. Aside from loving my new home, I fell in love with the community and my neighbors. Most of my neighbors had horses, and one day Jeannie called to invite me to the upcoming monthly ETI meeting at her home.

ETI stands for Equestrian Trails, Inc. The group's motto was, "Dedicated to the understanding of the horse." I attended meetings and got involved in the group and my community.

Within a couple of years, I became the ETI Corral President. It was such a gratifying time. This wonderful organization did many good things as a group for the equestrian community, such as supporting the Local Coastal Program, which protects laws that protect a homeowner's right to keep and ride horses in the Santa Monica Mountains. These rights have been systematically dwindling each year.

Corral 36 has come together in good times and in rough ones, bonding and getting to know each other better (sometimes kicking and screaming like mares do in a new herd). We helped another community, through the shared love of horses, by putting on fundraising events for the Compton Junior Posse. and continually attempted to expand our corral by bringing on new members in the community who love to ride. We grew our equestrian presence by working with the Santa Monica Parks & Recreation Department to restore the historical King Gillette Ranch facility to its original purpose including a stable, public arena, and riding trails. Additionally, we lobbied to keep the trails in the Santa Monica Mountains open and helped regulate the motorcycle and bike activity to increase safety for the equestrians.

Our ETI parties were notorious. They were mostly fundraisers for the corral but no one had more fun than we did! We would decorate our homes like a local saloon. My friend Holly, who rivaled Martha Stewart in the entertainment department, scored some inexpensive wallpaper with bottles that looked like a saloon's backdrop. We brought in gaming tables for the poker and gambling and we brought straw bales to surround the dance floor. We hired an amazing band and danced the night away, listening to the sounds of rock and country music with our horses whinnying in the background. It didn't get better than this.

We dressed up as dance hall girls with feathers, bustiers, and fishnet stockings, feeling sexy and having fun! As the guests arrived, I stood at the gate with a shot glass and a bottle of Patron.

"Welcome to the ranch," I'd say, pouring a shot and handing it to our guest. "Come and get your groove on."

These times bonded us and the community. We did good things and we had fun together.

* * * * *

It was to be a girls' trip. We had driven three hours north, trailering our horses to Ranch Oso in Morro Bay. I had gotten good at trailering by this time and we often went overnight camping with our horses. After unloading and getting the horses situated in their temporary stalls with hay and water, we unhooked the trailer and went to find our cabins. With my friend Abby sitting shotgun and Deb and Holly in the back, we set out to find our rooms. We drove down the narrow path and through the trees searching for cabin 366.

"I am hungry," I said.

"I am hot and tired," Abby said.

"I need a nap," Holly said.

"I need a drink," Deb said.

We slowed and circled. "362, 364, 369..." Abby said, reading the numbers on the cabin door. I circled again, moving slower. We circled three more times still not finding it and it was getting dark. We were all frustrated now.

"368..." Wait—how can it go from 369 back to 368? Something is wrong. On our third pass through the camp, we saw our friend Jeannie's truck and pulled up beside it.

"Let's go see Jeannie," I said. We jumped out of the truck and ran to their camper and found our friend with her three besties in the tiny trailer with a huge spread before them, sipping wine in chilled glasses and with a huge spread of various snacks in front of them. They were relaxed and happy, laughing and eating.

"We're lost," I said.

"We can't find our cabin," Deb said.

"They go up in increments of two," Jeannie said.

"Huh," I said, confused. "It must be there! Let's go, guys, we have to get settled before dark and the mess hall closes at 7 pm."

We piled back into the truck and set off once again. Finding 362, 364, and 369 …

"Okay, there is no 366," I said, and stopped in front of 369 and walked up to the door. As I looked at the number closer, I saw that the "9" was unattached and had fallen upside down! Mystery solved!

"This is it!" I cried out and opened the door. The girls jumped out of the truck and we happily ran inside the cabin. Since I was first through the door, I grabbed the room with the bathroom and a single bed.

"I've got mine," I said, leaving Deb and Abby to take the remaining second bedroom and Holly on the couch.

"Hey Darling, how did you snag the best room?" Deb asked.

"Oh," I replied, "I'm an only child—I don't share."

I still have not lived this down, but I'm happy to say we are all still friends.

The next morning, I woke up well-rested and happy. I was looking forward to our ride. We were taking a trail ride along a lake in the mountains.

"Good morning," I said cheerfully to my friends sitting at the kitchen table as I poured my coffee. "Ready to ride?"

"Ugh," my friend Deb said. "Abby thought she heard a

rat and kept me up all night."

"It wasn't a rat, it was a snake," Abby corrected her. "Something moved."

"Oh wow, you guys look tired," I said. "I slept great!"

"Yeah, no wonder," they said, exchanging glances.

An hour later, we had saddled up and joined 20 other riders who were participating in the ride. It seemed like the trail was straight up. We were tail to tail. It was hot. I was hot. I did not like riding in such close proximity to other riders. Neither did my horse! She may also have had only-child syndrome.

After a time, we saw the lake and were told to go single file and then gently ask our horses to swim across until we reached the shore. *What*, I thought? *I don't think Ditto knows how to swim.*

Holly, in front of me, expertly guided her horse, Sage, into and across the lake.

Huh, I thought, How hard could it be?

"Ok, Ditto," I said. "We got this."

I gathered the reins in my hand, lifted them up, and squeezed my legs, nudging her forward. She took a tentative step and I kept squeezing and kissing. Okay—we were gonna do this! We glided across the river, the water up to my waist. I could see the shore in front of me when suddenly, to my surprise, Ditto accelerated and moved out on her own to the other side. Without me! I went down. There was no horse under me. I was fully immersed under the water, not sure what was happening. When I came up, with water pouring out of my helmet, I could see Ditto in front of me, swimming forward, saddle and all to the other side and jumping out of the water. As I watched her stand there and shake the water off, I became aware of the laughter behind me. My friends were laughing uncontrollably.

"Darling," my friend Deb said, "All I could see when you came up was that your eyelashes were still perfectly on." They had been commenting on the fact that I had gotten eyelash extensions put on for the trip.

"It was brilliant!" Deb chuckled.

This is how I was dubbed Calamity Jane.

Retelling these lighthearted and fun stories keeps my friends and me bonded. Since those carefree days, my friends and I have experienced some dark, difficult things—divorce, death, and financial hardship. But the one common factor is that we all have come through it— stronger. So, although this chapter is titled "For the Love of the Horse," it might have been named "For the Love of the Horsewoman." The equestrian women I've had the pleasure to know are strong, resilient, and resourceful. I admire them and aspire to be like them.

My journey into the equestrian world has been rich and ever-changing. I have learned so much and met so many amazing people. I love the equine community and I love what horses do for our souls. I have attended many wonderful clinics led by such greats as Ray Hunt, Pat Parelli, Clint Anderson, Julie Goodnight, and Buck Brannaman. I learned to slow down in order to better communicate with my horses and I'm still working on becoming a better leader.

With the horses, my life became more relaxed. More down to earth. My favorite time was spent at home with the horses, brushing them, and doing ground exercises. My values shifted and I was no longer drawn to the city, spas, or shopping. I was content and happy at home. My friends were horsewomen like me. We all planned things we could do together while spending time with our horses. We had beautiful trails throughout the Santa Monica Mountains and we could go from one of our houses to the other and continue through the community to beautiful trails with ocean views. On holidays, we would dress up our horses and our tractors and participate in the local Fourth of July parade. We organized playdates and gymkhanas, doing things we had always wanted to do as children. We were living our dream.

It has been an interesting journey and I would not have traded it for the world. I have had years of horsekeeping now and I have made many of my life decisions around what is best for my horses. I've chosen where I will live and decided where I will go based on where I can afford a property to give the horses land to roam.

My horses are truly my family. My horse Ditto and I have been together for 19 years. She was six years old when we met, and now she is 30. We became volunteer mounted patrol officers together. As a team, we had to pass a rigorous training course, and it was very gratifying when we did. I was proud of us both. Part of our duties were to ride and patrol our parks and help others in need or keep a look out for wrongdoing. Not long after we got signed up, a local girl went missing and we were a part of the team combing the hills looking for her.

I became a certified equine therapist in 2014. While in my basic EAGALA training on the beautiful island of Hilo, Hawaii, I bonded with a very beautiful chestnut bay gelding. We were at the far side of the field alone, standing quietly. I was in awe of his beauty and my gaze was concentrated on his face. We began to look into each other's eyes and I saw a tear forming and slowly slide from its eye. Seeing this and watching this horse cry made me get in touch with the feelings I'd been holding back and I began to cry. This horse helped me release years of pent-up anger and pain I'd been carrying since my divorce. The feelings of shame, remorse, and sadness just came up and flowed out of me. After that session, I was a believer in equine therapy.

Equine therapy can have a very positive influence on trauma patients, vets, and addicts. I cannot think of a day or situation where time with a horse does not make it better.

In my coaching practice, I offer sessions where clients spend time with my horses in the arena to help heal childhood trauma through our equine therapy classes. My clients enter the corral, sit on the mounting block, and wait to see which horse approaches them. They allow the horse to communicate with them for a while, and then we discuss the feelings that came up for them. This therapeutic exercise is very insightful and beneficial.

Time spent with my horses and horse people have been some of the best experiences of my life. I look back fondly and smile at the thought of the master negotiator who managed to get two horses when buying a house and also convinced the seller to "throw in" the horse trailer.

CHAPTER 13

Road to Recovery

After my third divorce, I was living in a spacious guest house on a lovely avocado and lemon farm that I rented in a rural area that was only 20 minutes from my mom. Now in her mid-80s, I wanted to be close by if she needed my help. My horses were on the property with me and it was lush and beautiful and we were happy. The property was only an hour from my friends in Santa Barbara, so I had the choice to socialize or stay home and meditate (I mean isolate).

* * * * *

It was Tuesday at 11 am. My phone rang and I looked at the readout.

"Hi Vic," I said, "It's been a while!"

My dear friend had moved to northern California to set up a restaurant at a high-end resort and I hadn't seen her in ages.

"I'm so sorry," she said.

"For what?" I asked, confused.

"That Raymond passed."

"What are you talking about?" I asked in a loud shrill voice.

"I saw it on a Facebook post this morning," she said.

"I'll call you back," I said hurriedly and quickly opened my social media. Victoria was always the one who broke the latest news to me. She was connected and always knew things that no one else did. She was the one who had called me that September morning at 7:30 am when the plane crashed into the second tower.

There it was. The post showed my love, Raymond, looking up and smiling as he blew out his birthday cake. But, this was a picture from a year before. This year he had been in the hospital on his birthday, in a coma suffering from COVID. He died one day after his 73rd birthday. It was a complete shock. He was taken too soon. He thought he'd live forever. He assured me on more than one occasion not to worry, because he had longevity in his genes and we still had time to be together. He believed that he would have time to finish out his chapter with Candace because she was 84, and then he'd spend his last chapter with me. However, it was not to be. I don't regret looking him up and beginning again after such a long time. I wish that it had been a different outcome, but I know that I will see him again one day and we will finish the dance. Until then, I know that he is in the clouds, taking beautiful images and smiling down on those he loves.

I put my head down on my desk and cried. Cried for my lost love, for my hope of having another chance at love, and for the state of the world and the scary unknown.

I took a deep breath and looked around me. There was nothing left for me here. Romantically speaking, there was not a single man left on the planet who cared if I was alive or not. I was completely alone and ready for a change.

After COVID, I no longer felt at home on the avocado ranch where I rented. My $6,000 per month overhead was too high and it was not sustainable. I didn't know when I would make another real estate deal, so I was on a quest to get safe. I needed to move and went back to my search for a less expensive place to live where I could bring my three dogs and three horses.

On weekends, I would cruise the outlying areas and look for properties. I'd fallen in love with the idea of remodeling a mobile home. I'd been flipping houses for many years and I was intrigued by how much space and comfort you could get in a mobile home for a fraction of the price. I knew that others would appreciate this fact too if I could only find some money to invest.

* * * * *

One day, my best friend told me of a place that her daughter had recently moved to called Ridgecrest. It was in southern California up the I-395 on the way to Mammoth. She invited me to come see it. Deb's daughter always had loads of animals, and like me, needed lots of land. It was the weekend and I decided to go check out her new ranch. I'd once done a real estate deal there, so I knew of Ridgecrest, but it had been years since I'd been there. It was a nice way to spend a Saturday. After I drove for what seemed like hours on the desolate two-lane highway where all I saw were stark mountains on either side, I saw the sign for Ridgecrest.

With the help of my GPS, I took the turnoff, found the property, and met my friend Deb, her husband John, and another man they introduced to me as Mike. Mike had a huge, beautiful smile that could light up the room, and he could sell ice to an Eskimo as the saying goes. I liked the fact that Taz moved here, thinking that my friend would drive out here to visit her daughter, so I'd know someone in the area and I'd have a friend that would visit occasionally. Mike said there were lots of opportunities in the nearby town of Inyokern and recommended that I check it out.

At home on my computer, I googled it and in an area that was otherwise barren, I saw a patch of green on my Google Earth and zoomed in for a closer look. Green pastures of hay and clusters of green trees and horse trailers! Score! I had found my spot. I learned that

Inyokern is where they had filmed *Top Gun*. If it was good enough for Maverick, it was good enough for me!

The next day, I called Mike and told him my thoughts. He said that he had bought his truck in Inyokern from one of the neighbors. He gave me the address and I looked it up on my computer and began to search for the ownership. I sent letters to each of the out-of-town owners in the neighborhood and wrote that I would like to buy their property. About a week later, I got a call from the owner of the corner piece I'd been looking at.

"Yeah, this is Bob. Heard you were looking for me."

"Hi Bob, my name's Deborah and I'm looking for some land—is yours for sale?" I asked.

"Well, everything except my family and my soul is for sale at the right price."

So, I offered a price, and he accepted, and the rest is history, as they say. Luckily, I had enough cash from my last commission for the down payment and the owner agreed to carry the rest himself. Bob had bought this property in a tax sale and had never actually been to see it.

And just like that, I had bought 15 acres in a community of 900 people in the Mojave Desert, two and a half hours from my friends and family. This was progress—a new adventure. Surely, I thought that with a mortgage payment of $635 per month, I'd be able to afford myself and would not need to worry about finding a man to support me.

Sadly, reducing my overhead by more than half was still not enough for me to be solvent, let alone financially secure. The property had no water and no electricity, and the mobile home had no ceiling, walls, or floor. The title report deemed it, "no value." But it had value to me and I was determined to make it my home.

All of the money I had left went into making this old mobile home livable again and safe from the elements. It was not a task for the weak-hearted.

At first, I saw it as a project as if I was a contestant on an episode of *Survivor*. I had brought my 40' shipping container with me, which had a bed and a TV in it. This was my temporary new home. At night my dogs and I would hole up together in the little container using a generator to run the fan and TV, and I had battery-operated candles. I had a hospital toilet with a bucket under it that I used and dumped daily, rinsed, and repeated. In the morning, I would plug my Keurig coffee maker into the outside generator to make coffee and oatmeal. It was loud, but it worked.

I had an ice chest that stored cream, yogurt, fruit, and butter. It was perfect. I had an outside table that I had brought with me, where I prepared the salad, rotisserie chicken, and canned green beans I'd bought at the store. We were good. My dogs looked at me and wondered when this new adventure was going to end and they could get back to their pampered, air-conditioned life.

It was spring when we arrived and we were trying to beat the heat. Little by little, the façade of the city wore off. My hair was in a braid and I stopped wearing makeup.

I did not unpack any of the boxes from my move for the first year. I only wore the clothes that were packed in my dresser drawers. Jeans, T-shirts and baseball hats.

My workers came from Los Angeles, two hours away, and they would stay for four days, working on the property from sunup to sundown. I worked alongside them, doing demolition, driving to Home Depot to get and pay for supplies, driving to get my crew lunch, and taking them to dinner at night.

Within two days, my industrious team had the ceiling on the trailer restored and they began to work on the walls. Within a few weeks, I had a secure place where I could escape the elements. Each morning we rose with the sun, had coffee and fruit, and started our day working until dusk.

The original owners, Marv and Virginia, had died here in the '80s and this property had been abandoned since then. Their family had come here and ransacked the home, taking what they wanted and throwing the rest of their parents' belongings outside on the dirt to become a new home for the rats, rabbits, and ravens. Looking through the pile of their past life, I found an old calendar and their family checkbook from 1987. I felt a connection with them and was saddened that their life had been discarded and laid bare for anyone to see. It was not lost on me that this could one day be my story. I made a vow to let go of things that I don't need and things that I'm not using regularly.

It was 115 degrees when the sun went down. It was said

to be the hottest summer this valley had seen in 20 years.

Wow, I thought to myself, *could you have picked a hotter place?* I'd basically put my finger on a map and moved there. The house was livable, but there was no electricity, so no air conditioning or fans. My dear friend Lynn, even though she was still angry at me for moving this far away, sent me ice packs to use at night so that I could sleep. I kept them in my ice chest and used them on me and my dogs to keep us comfortable.

My friends are shocked that I am here. Out in this desert. Alone. I'm a girly girl. I'm used to lunches in Beverly Hills and bi-weekly mani-pedis, lashes, and facials. It is not that I chose this place for its beauty or amenities. This was what I could afford. My "why" is my animals. I needed a place where I could afford them and us, and be okay. If I did not have my animals, I would have made different choices. I came here so that I would have enough land that they could roam and live out their days relaxed and happy.

After leaving the city, moving to this remote and raw land, living on it for six months without water or electricity, and living through the extreme seasons for two years, I will always feel secure in my ability to settle anywhere and recreate myself with little or nothing. I now know how to live on less. I know how to be alone. I know how to be resourceful. I like my own company. I am strong and creative and find joy in simple things.

I made a decision to live in the present and look at each

moment to see what brings me joy. Asking myself, "Does this fill me up?" Even though this location was not my first choice, I have come to love the land and myself. I've gained respect for my resiliency, resourcefulness, and determination.

There is a strength that comes from having the confidence that we are capable of taking care of ourselves. That is not to say I've done it alone. Anything but. God has been with me every step of the way.

I'm reminded of the story of the man who was walking on the beach and cried out to God, "Where were you when I needed you?"

God replied, "My child, I've been with you the entire time."

"No," the man cried, "I only see one set of footprints in the sand."

And God answered, "Yes, my son, most of the way, I have been carrying you."

God has carried me here and God has shown me such grace. He has sent amazing people to help me on my journey.

There were the neighbors who sent a port-a-potty as a housewarming gift. The neighbor who sent a generator. The neighbor who sent a solar trailer when I had no electricity. The neighbor who helped me when the wind blew my fence down.

The neighbor who came with rat traps when the mice came. The neighbor who re-homed the rattlesnake I found, the family who brought me rakes and umbrellas for shade, the friends who gave me chickens, and the friend who sent me ice packs so that my dogs and I could sleep in the 115-degree heat.

The friend who Zelled me cash when I had no money for gas. The strangers in the grocery store who paid my bill when I didn't have enough to cover the cost. I've been carried every step of the way. Seek and you shall find. I am blessed and highly favored.

My friends consider me lucky. But I know and understand that it is not luck that brings me all of my good fortune. Rather, it is that I plug into God and the power of the universe and know that all is available to me.

I practice daily, and sometimes hourly, the following mantras:

I am blessed and highly favored.

Vast amounts of money come to me from various sources on a continuous basis.

I use these mantras interchangeably to draw my energy higher and to program myself to expect God's blessings.

So much has been given to me that I sometimes can't comprehend it. I went from not having enough to eat to having a family friend give me a house. Yes, they just gave it to me. Because they could and because they wanted to.

It was a usual workday and I was at my desk reviewing a lease when my phone rang.

"This is Deborah," I said, pushing the accept button on my phone.

"Ruthe wants to talk to you," Ruthe's office manager, Rose, said on the line.

"Sure," I said. "Put her on."

"Deborita," my client said, her musical lilt making me smile. "How are things in the desert?"

"Hot," I said, and we laughed.

"Seriously, are you doing okay?"

"Yes, all is well," I said reassuringly. My friends had worried since I'd packed up and moved to this isolated locale.

"Listen," she began, "Lucy is moving. We bought her a house a year ago and she got a job up north, so we want to gift her house to you."

"What?" I said, not understanding.

"Yes—we want to give this house to you."

"Why don't you sell it?" I asked. "I can clean it up and rent it out for you."

"No," she said. "It's yours. Do what you want with it."

We made small talk and then said our goodbyes and I hung up the phone, stunned. I had just gone from wondering how I was going to pay for hay to having a house that I could sell or rent out. What a miracle God had provided. I was still reaping benefits from this generous family that continued to show their appreciation for the real estate benefits we had created when we worked together. They were a blessing in my life and their generosity never failed to leave me speechless.

These are the types of philanthropists who really want

to make a difference in their friends' lives. They walk the talk. Every day. I'm still trying to find a way to become the type of person who gives like that. Gives without strings attached or thoughts of what can be gained. Giving and then forgetting that it was given.

Each morning when I wake up and walk outside, the cool, crisp air hits me and I am struck by the beautiful immensity of the Sierra Nevada Mountain range that borders my property. I catch my breath at the beauty before me. These mountains stretch the entire length of my property and I feel as though they are mine. It is winter and the clouds hang low and cast shadows on the peaks and crevices. They change with the season and the time of day. The patterns are unique and ever-changing. I feel blessed to witness this slice of nature.

At this moment, I see at least 20 black ravens, the size of cats, sitting around my horses at the corral, convening and conversing, presumably about their plans for the day. I begin feeding my horses. Grabbing an armful of hay and placing it in each of their 100-gallon buckets. I watch them happily munching away as I fill their water buckets and then move on to let my chickens out of their coop and spread their breakfast, which includes leftovers from my dinner the night before, along with their mixture of corn, oats, and sunflower seeds.

I notice a family of white doves sitting high on the branches of a dead tree and I muse at how once, years ago, I paid someone to bring doves like this to my wedding to be released from a box at the end of the ceremony. Did they fly all the way home to somewhere like this? And now, here, I see them for free every day. I feel blessed by the wildlife all around me. It is a gift and I'm grateful. This is my Zen. God is speaking to me through these souls. The message I'm hearing is, "All is well. You are okay."

I'd only been in my new isolation a short time. This is the most extreme I'd gone before. Isolating myself two and a half hours away from family and friends. Speaking to no one except my animals. I was now free to listen to the voice within. I am not unhappy here.

I began to notice the changing colors of the amazing mountain range that graced my property line and I began to look for signs from God. I made peace with the heat and the wind. The ants and the immense amount of dirt weren't great either, but those were a lesser irritation.

When my internet worked, I was happy. I could watch TV and check my emails. I needed to be able to keep my routine and work remotely. Without the internet, I'd be lost. I was never bored. There was always something to do. I had a schedule and a routine that I stuck to. I woke with the sun and the sound of a crowing rooster. I got up each morning, let my dogs out, and stretched my arms to the sky, thanking God for the day. Next, I turned on the water and walked to my horses to feed and water them. I returned, made coffee, checked my emails, and watched my YouTube how-to videos for 30 minutes on how to build a shed. Then I fed the dogs and myself. Got dressed and turned on my computer. Time to work.

I'd only been here about six months, after having spent a chunk of my money getting the corrals and the old barn restored for my horses. Then, just when I thought it was safe and secure, we had 50 mph winds. The house shook like I was on a moving train. I had to push the couch against the doors because they felt like they were going cave in.

The next morning, I went outside to survey the damage. A tree had fallen, and so had my gate. Solar panels had flown off the trailer and broke. The roof came completely off the barn. It was terrifying! Thankfully, the horses were not hit by the flying metal roof panels, but we needed hard hats from all of the debris flying through the air. Also, the electricity in the well went out so there was no water for the horses. I needed a backup plan! This was my introduction to rural living!

Through necessity, I became super resourceful. I began to see that every item I had could be used for something else. I saw a dual purpose in everything. I noticed that products that were selling on Amazon were often just re-purposed from something else someone used previously. I began to multipurpose everything. Just like my grandparents had modeled this behavior when I was growing up, I finally understood.

An empty can was now used as a measuring device at the chicken coop. An empty toilet paper roll was the perfect seed starter in my garden. All food scraps went to the chickens or compost. All dead plants went to the compost pile. The water that dripped from the faucet had a dog bowl under it. The wire on the property went around the plants to keep the rabbits out. The tattered tarps found on the property from years gone past found a second life on top of the coops for shade to keep the chickens cool. The moving blankets that were left behind were wrapped around the pipes in the winter. My former dog's collar was used to keep a gate closed from predators. Excess wood was put across two cement blocks to make a shelf. An old air-conditioner shell was a nesting box for my hens.

An abandoned freezer on the property was used as a raised bed to grow vegetables. Everything was used and nothing was wasted. It was an exciting way to see things. I was becoming self-sufficient and realizing that I didn't need to run to the store each time I needed something. I used my imagination and YouTube. I saw how the people who lived here 30 years ago did things.

The former owner used the wire from a coat hanger to make clips to hold things up. He didn't need to go to Home Depot to buy wire for a project. He used what he had. I learned how a chain link fence was made and I built a fence using the old pipe and chain links on the property.

As my new life unfolded, each day was a new adventure. One day, as my movers were transferring the last of my things from the huge moving van to a POD in front of my dilapidated mobile home, a car stopped outside my gate. I walked over to the old beat-up Toyota and a man smiled at me and said, "Hey, it's about to get hot here, you're gonna need some solar."

I had just had a few weekends of flaky electricians not calling me back and random handymen trying to get the well to work so I was tired of having people on my property.

"I'm good," I said. "I'm staying in the container."

"You don't get it," he said. "It will be 115 soon and you're gonna die out here."

"Oh…" was all I could muster out.

"I'm gonna bring one of my solar trailers over," he said, the matter settled.

"Okay," I nodded. "Uh…thanks."

The next day, true to his word, he rolled up in a white F350 work truck, pulling a strange-looking trailer with solar panels fastened all around it. My neighbor, whose name I learned was Joe, got out of the truck, set up the solar device for me, and said, "Just keep it awhile and use it—no worries, I have a bunch of them."

This contraption became my best friend for the next three months and saved my life. I was able to set up my office and it ran my internet, computer, plug-in light, and even the refrigerator that my handyman had brought me from a yard sale in LA.

Some days, I would ask, "Lord, why am I here?" I am alive. I am on this planet. I am healthy and strong, yet I have no purpose. I thought fixing this house was my purpose, but I am out of money. I can't keep going into debt for this.

God told me to get out of my self-pity and take the next right action. So, I stood up and dusted myself off. I went to the riding class at my neighbor's property and I saw all of the like-minded people who loved horses like me. They had saddled and mounted up, wind and all. They and their horses were oblivious to the strong gusts blowing around them. Sitting in the shade of the massive elm tree with Callie, the instructor, and watching the horses go through the lesson, I realized that all was well, and I was relaxed and happy. I began to think of this place as my home.

Next, I went to the market to get supplies for my lunch, and returning home I sat and ate and realized that I was right where I needed to be—all was well. I cleared out two bags of stuff that I had carried here from the move. Cosmetic supplies that I rarely used and barely needed. In two huge bags of stuff, I had not found the one thing I was looking for—deodorant. Believe me, I needed it. We carry so much baggage with us that we don't need and we often overlook the one thing that we do.

It is important to feel our feelings. Process them and get them up and out. But we do not need to let them guide our actions. We do not feel our way into "right action." We act ourselves into doing what is right for our greater good and then we can feel better. At a point, we will look up at the continuous right actions we have taken and we will feel good about ourselves. We will feel grateful, we will feel happy, we will feel proud and accomplished. Only by taking the next right action of putting down the addiction, whether it is food or spending money you don't have, or continuing to let a man control you or mess with your feelings, will you begin to strengthen the muscle of self-worth and love. Esteemable actions bring self-esteem.

After returning home from the feedstore, I shifted the truck into park and grabbed the wheelbarrow. Realizing that there was no one around but me to unload, one by one, I slowly slid each heavy bag of feed off the truck bed down into the old wheelbarrow. Once inside the coop, I hoisted each 50-pound bag of oats for my chickens up into the metal can. In this solitary task, I felt a surge of pride in the strength I'd developed through tending to my land. No helping hands were nearby, so I had to use my fortitude.

I have learned to navigate obstacles with ingenuity, discovering workarounds and leveraging techniques. Sometimes improvisation became key. I'd stack bricks that I found on the land to fashion an impromptu platform, enabling me to ease the bags onto a step up and into the empty metal container. Slow, but sure, I always found a way.

That task completed, I sat on the nearby stump to rest and watched my contented chickens pecking happily at their meal. I began to reflect on the countless remarkable women I'd met in my life since moving here: the pipefitter who deftly crafted the pipes from my well; the commanding presence of the officer on the nearby military base who led a team in the intricacies of ballistics and weaponry, building bombs; the compassionate neighbor who came with her .22 to ease my dog's suffering and skillfully operated a backhoe to lay him to rest.

Even the painter who transformed my walls and the neighbor who patiently imparted knowledge of securing a tarp on a roof using zip ties before the impending rain— both women. Lastly, the woman who taught me how to install and maintain an electric fence.

These experiences underscored a vital truth: male companionship is welcome, but not a prerequisite for strength or capability. I have embraced a "get 'er done" attitude, armed with nothing more than determination, resources like YouTube, and the willingness to learn through trial and error. I can impress myself.

* * * * *

My new home looked like an unfinished construction site. I was overwhelmed by what to do with all the stuff I had. I looked around at the piles of stuff I'd brought with me and had paid thousands of dollars to move here. To a place where the things have no home. They sat around in various piles representing unfinished projects. Deals I had started but didn't complete. Boxes of china and crystal from days gone by when I used to host parties and all of the family get-togethers. I still held the hope that I would find a home for these beloved things.

As I looked around and "saw" all of the things I've been holding on to, I realized they are placeholders. They are reminders of where I'd been, who I was, or what I was doing at the time. But they were just collecting dust. They were no longer relevant to who I was now or where I was going. I needed to look forward. I needed to set my sights on who I was becoming. If I was interested in anything, I could Google it. What I was interested in right now was understanding who I was. What kind of person I was and what I could contribute to the world I was living in.

I began by taking one box at a time. I would open the box and remove each item in it one by one. I would hold the object, look at it, and ask myself, "Is this useful to me now?" Do I need it? Do I want it? Could someone else use it? I tried to be discriminating. I found the shower caddy that would be helpful in the RV I was using for my workers. I found the bowls I used daily and used them over and over and did not unpack any kitchen things. I found the towels and put them in the appropriate room.

I knew these "things" were stressing me out, so why were they so hard to get rid of? Why couldn't I just take them to Goodwill and drop them off? Old work files, books that were 20 years old, pictures, cards, etc.

When I struggled with letting an item go, I read the "Change Me" prayer. In her book, *It's Not Your Money*, Tosha Silver instructs us to say a prayer before we begin the clearing process. "… *Let everything that needs to go, go. Let everything that needs to come, come. I am utterly Your own. You are Me. I am You. We are One.*"

Doing this brought me into the present and I could

relax. I was able to let go of possessions that were no longer useful to the person I was now or the person I was meant to be.

My good friend Karen is very good at "editing" things out of her life. She does not cling, covet, or hoard. She moves things through and keeps her space open and serene. This minimalist is a deeply loving person who knows and values what is truly important in life. She doesn't cling to things but to people, whom she holds dear and close to her, whether they have been useful in her life or not. If she loves them, that is enough. They are hers forever.

Karen gave me a beautiful cashmere coat that I'd kept for years. Letting go of this coat is bittersweet. I realize that it is from an era past. One that will never be returned or repeated. As I pull it from its box closet and hold it up, I see a very tiny hole most likely made by a moth. A flaw barely recognizable to the naked eye and yet it is indicative of the length of time this coat has been in service. The following is from a blog I posted called "Edit your Life."

Today, I said goodbye to an old friend. I am releasing a coat that I had hanging in my closet back at home for more than 20 years. This was longer than most relationships. It was given to me by another old friend, a dear one. It was an ankle-length navy blue trench coat with a brown faux fur full-length liner. It had belts at the waist and buckles at the sleeves. This coat represented my old friend: chic, hip, lovely, expensive, irreplaceable. A coat that I never would have bought for myself. I was only in an economic condition that I felt I could afford such a purchase for a short period of my life. And apparently, this time has never occurred in the winter because I never purchased an expensive coat for myself. It must have felt frivolous to me. The few expensive frivolous things I have spent my money on are designer sunglasses and a Prada handbag. So, an article of clothing such as this one that I did not feel was in my league was always a treasured and coveted thing when given to me by this close friend. I wanted to be just like her and have everything she had.

But having hosted this coat for such a long time, I realized that it held a place in my heart but was not serving any purpose in my life. It rarely gets cold enough to use it and its time has passed. But it is still in pristine condition and it is time to pass it along to someone who may actually use it and love it like I have.

I was looking at some old pictures taken of my friend and me when we were in our prime and remembered the feelings of those days. Life is simpler now, the highs not as high and the lows not as low, not chemically altered by synthetic assistance. But the feeling of letting the coat go feels freeing, like I'm making room for the new. I'm telling the universe to "bring it." The unknown. I'm open and I'm ready.

* * * * *

In my 20s, I was a student of life. I attended every seminar and clinic I could on self-help, self-awareness, etc. Now, having much experience under my belt, I want to give back and be a bridge between life experience and what is holding someone back, if it will help someone else avoid the pain and pitfalls that I had to go through.

Moving lock, stock, and barrel out of town was expensive. I had a cash flow problem and was trying to get safe. But as I looked around I saw that I had a lot of things that had value and yet did not fit into my new life. I put them on Facebook Marketplace, Offer Up, and Ebay. I wasn't getting the response I wanted so I put them on my Facebook page. That is where I had the most success. My Facebook friends stepped up, and I'm so grateful for their support!

My friend Deb likes to say, "It takes a village, darling." She is so right.

My village gave me support, encouragement, cash, and love. They cheered me on in my new venture and I am truly grateful. I don't know where this journey will lead me, but it has taught me so much. I came here on a whim and I learned lessons I didn't know that I needed to learn. I got stronger. My faith grew. I became happy. I want to thank friends and family and remarkably, strangers who stepped up in a way that totally humbled me.

This land speaks to me. I'm having a love affair with each creature and new blade of grass I see. The property has become a sort of wildlife sanctuary. Each species knows they are safe here and won't be harmed. Even the coyotes seem to understand that if they leave my animals alone, we will leave them alone. The family of ravens that have adopted this property have become my guards to keep predators away from my chickens and little 12-pound Schnoodle, Chloe. They love to sit on the barn roof or corral gate, squawk at me, and then fly overhead in formation to entertain me. The droves of wild cottontail rabbits, hawks, and wild doves all sit on the abandoned branches and survey their sanctuary. Snakes curl up under the greasewood shrubs, seeking shade, waiting until night to go to work to keep the rat population down. A lone sunflower pokes its head up through an abandoned tire that hasn't seen water for a year.

Everywhere I look, nature is putting on a beautiful show for me, and I'm so grateful that I discovered this majestic place that sustained me and made me resilient and strong. This land is my refuge in the storm and will remain a haven for me for my future. I have created my own safety net and there is nothing more gratifying than that.

Now, I don't ask God why I am here. I just ask him to show me his will for me TODAY. I'm very lucky to still be here. I know that I have a purpose and I believe that purpose is to give back.

Progress, not perfection. Moving to the desert didn't cure all of my problems. I was still me and had the same issues as before, and they required attention and work to heal. It is okay to slip and fall back into old habits. It is natural. We are human. We stumble and we may fall. The trick is to get up, dust yourself off, and begin again.

Forgive yourself and others and just start over. I thought that I was cured. I thought that I had it all together. That I had neutrality over food. That my relationships were all healthy. That my money situation was healthy. But like all addiction, it is not cured. It is only managed by doing what works one day at a time.

There will be setbacks. Let go of perfection. It's okay. I know what I'm striving for and I will keep reaching for that without punishing myself. I'm doing my best. That's enough. I have enough. I do enough. I am enough. You're enough. Thank you, Lord, I will find my joy today. All is well and you are on your throne. LIFE IS GOOD.

Men, money, and food were my addictions of the past, but I can say that I am now recovering from the obsession with them. I no longer act out in these areas. When I practice the tools I've been given, I am granted a daily reprieve. I no longer have to hurt myself with men, money, or food. I am not dating and sometimes I do get lonely, but it is short-lived. I know that someday I will have a healthy and fulfilling relationship. If he was sent by God and it felt right, I'd welcome it, but for now, I'm enjoying a relationship with myself. My money situation is sane and I use my budget and make wise choices. I live within my monthly income while attempting to grow my passive income and my food is in its place. It is weighed, measured, and delicious. I'm in a healthy body that I love and one that has been so, so good to me. I am satisfied.

CHAPTER 14

The Fix: There is a Solution

Men, money, and food. These three things have derailed me in my past. The men were about trying to gain love and repair the trauma of my relationship with my emotionally withholding stepfather; the money was to make myself feel worthwhile; and the food was used to cope with both. Of course, I loved food and all of the celebrations that involved food, but I began to use it as a drug to cope with the struggles with men, trying to feel loved, and the stress around trying to make and keep money. Then, when I would eat, I would overeat, and it would activate the cycle of self-loathing when I could not control it. These three things are behind most of the angst in my life.

In my early twenties, I was in so much pain after learning that I was illegitimate, and I was on a quest for answers to find inner peace. That is how I began my personal growth journey in the '90s and found the 12-step program of Codependents Anonymous (CODA). I attended meetings and learned what was meant by codependency. I needed to find freedom and peace from the conflict and tension I was having in my personal relationships. I learned how the painful traumas of my family of origin and the emptiness of my childhood were causing me pain. I realized how my history was causing me to act out in certain ways. This was where I first learned about the 12 steps. I learned how following these principles in all my affairs would help me overcome my self-defeating ways. This was the start of my lifelong pursuit of personal growth. This program gave me hope, strength, and tools to live my life the way God intended me to be—joyous, precious, and free.

When I read the CODA pamphlet to determine if I related to the patterns of Codependency, this is what I found:

My good feelings about who I am stem from being liked by you.

My good feelings about who I am stem from receiving your approval.

Your struggle affects my serenity. My mental attention focuses on solving your problems or relieving your pain.

My mental attention is focused on pleasing you.

My mental attention is focused on protecting you.

My mental attention is focused on manipulating you (to do it my way).

My self-esteem is bolstered by solving your problems.

My self-esteem is bolstered by relieving your pain.

My own hobbies are put aside. My time is spent sharing your interests and hobbies.

Your clothing and personal appearance are dictated by my desires as I feel you are a reflection of me.

Your behavior is dictated by my desires as I feel you are a reflection of me.

I am not aware of how I feel, I am aware of how you feel.

I am not aware of what I want, I ask what you want, I am not aware, I assume.

The dreams I have for my future are linked to you.

My fear of rejection determines what I say or do.

I use giving as a way of feeling safe in our relationship.

My social circle diminishes as I involve myself with you.

I put my values aside in order to connect with you.

I value your opinion and way of doing things more than my own.

The quality of my life is in relation to the quality of yours.

The typical characteristics of a codependent are:

I assume responsibility for others' feelings and/or behaviors.

I feel overly responsible for others' feelings and/or behaviors.

I have difficulty in identifying feelings. Am I angry?

Lonely? Sad? Happy? Joyful?

I have difficulty expressing feelings. Am I feeling happy, sad, hurt, joyful?

I tend to fear and/or worry about how others may respond to my feelings.

I have difficulty in forming and/or maintaining close relationships.

I am afraid of being hurt and/or rejected by others.

I am a perfectionist and place too many expectations on myself and others.

I have difficulty in making decisions.

I tend to minimize, alter, or even deny the truth about how I feel.

Other people's actions and attitudes tend to determine how I react or respond. I tend to put other people's wants and needs first.

My fear of others' feelings (anger) determines what I say and do.

I question or ignore my own values to connect with significant others. I value others' opinions more than my own.

My self-esteem is bolstered by outer or other influences. I cannot acknowledge good things about myself.

My serenity and mental attention are determined by how others are feeling and/or behaving.

I tend to judge everything I do, think, or say harshly, by someone else's standards. Nothing is done, said, or thought "Good Enough."

I do not know or believe that being vulnerable and asking for help is both okay and normal.

I do not know that it is okay to talk about the problems outside the family or that feelings just are, and it is better to share them than to deny, minimize, or justify them.

I tend to put other people's wants and needs before my own.

I am steadfastly loyal. Even if the loyalty is unjustified and personally harmful.

I have to feel needed to have relationships with others.

Once we identify and relate, we can determine how to change.

In his book, *The Six Pillars of Self-Esteem*, Nathaniel Branden wrote that the six practices that form our self-esteem are: living consciously, self-acceptance, self-responsibility, self-assertiveness, living purposefully, and personal integrity.

I assert that the most important aspect of the above is self-acceptance. That is to love ourselves. In our early years, we might have gotten the message that we are not enough, and we spend our entire lives trying to turn this around and need to learn to love ourselves and others. I use the mantra, "I love and approve of myself" over and over and over again, many times a day, to override the feeling of being less than and having self-doubt in my life.

I wrote this book to detail the traumas in my life that may have contributed to the development of my addictions and to discuss the reasons I medicated myself with various things to avoid the shame that I carried with me. If I can help one person to know that they are not alone and that there is a solution, I will be happy.

When I married, I hadn't healed my past shame and trauma. I just continued to mask them, which is why I continued to act out. What I've learned now is that we are as sick as our secrets. I no longer need to hide from my past. I need only to accept what has happened, forgive myself and others, and move on. Stay in the day and do the next right action.

Whether you use sex, love, alcohol, drugs, or drama to cope with your past trauma, if these things are holding you back and you want to overcome them, just know that there is a way through it to the other side.

In his book, *Man's Search for Meaning,* written in the '50s after his time in a concentration camp, Viktor Frankl determined that our happiness boils down to knowing our "why." In his book, he quoted Nietzsche, saying, "He who has a 'why' to live, can bear almost any 'how.'" It is the *pursuit* of something that has meaning for us, not necessarily obtaining it. When we are pursuing or chasing our dreams, we get outside of ourselves and stop focusing on our low-level desires and negative emotions. Therefore, when I am pursuing my business and growing my income, I take the focus off how much money I currently have and rather stay in the pursuit of giving more service in my business, which increases my satisfaction.

Once I found and began to work a program, my life

began to improve. I just needed an action plan. Action is what saves us. Yoga, meditation, journaling, affirmations, and expressing gratitude are tools we can use. We all need to find something outside ourselves that we can surrender to. Something to turn our will over to. A higher power. I call mine God—some say it's an acronym for the Gift of Desperation. Even if we don't consider ourselves religious, when we are desperate, most of us turn to God. "God, please help me with this" or "God, please help me with that." When we are at our wit's end, we turn to someone besides ourselves. We turn it over. We surrender.

We must take responsibility for our lives. We all have circumstances and we all get to choose how we respond to these circumstances. Our response or perspective is what makes the difference between our misery and our happiness. We can choose to remain neutral on the event that happened and we can choose to take the next right action toward the desired goal and leave the results to God.

Once I learned that I was responsible for my life, I began to grow up and my life began to improve.

I have been a student of various teachings throughout history. The Universal Truths. These messages come in various forms, but they all have a similar message. Beginning with the Bible, the Torah, and later the Koran. The 12 steps are adapted from these teachings. We just need to follow these basic principles and our lives will be transformed.

My daily practices are as follows (based on the "Just

for Today" pamphlet):

Upon waking each morning, I take a deep breath in, and as I slowly exhale, I breathe out and repeat the mantra, "Thank you, Thank you, Thank you." Next, I ask God to show me his plan for me and to guide my steps. I say the prayer, "Your will not mine be done."

Next, I stay in the day, stay in the NOW. I don't look down the road. I stay in the Here and Now and take the next right action. Anytime I get ahead of myself, the worry and stress begin. In the past, when the stress came, I would medicate myself. Now I slow down, breathe, take the next right action, and don't worry about the outcome. It will take care of itself.

Next, I do my best to keep a good attitude (pleasing personality). In his book *The Laws of Success*, Napoleon Hill cites this as one of the universal laws. This means to be happy. As the song says, *Don't worry—be happy!* It is so true. We must keep a pleasing personality and spread that to others. When we are in this state, we raise our vibration and the universe conspires with us to make our dreams and desires come true.

Acceptance: As the Serenity Prayer in the Big Book says, we ask for the serenity to accept the things we cannot change, to find the courage to change what we can, and the wisdom to know the difference. It is what it is. Accept reality or change it. It doesn't need to be an emotional struggle filled with drama. Pray to do your best and let go of it.

Emotions are my Kryptonite! I cannot afford to focus on people who constantly have drama or problems and I cannot allow distractions or fantasies to derail me.

Strengthen your mind: We need to concentrate on and show up for something on a daily basis that used to baffle us or be over our heads. When we slow down and break it down, we will amaze ourselves with how much we can understand. We are living in an unprecedented time. We can Google, and we can YouTube things and find our way. It is unbelievable what we can achieve if we only try.

We must stretch our souls: We must connect with the GOD of our understanding on a regular basis. I start each day by saying a daily prayer: "God, I offer myself to thee to do with me as thou wilt. Take away my difficulties so that others may see the power of your glory and love. Relieve me of the bondage of self so that I may better do thy will. Thy will, not mine, be done. Amen." Then, I do a half hour of quiet time or meditation in the morning before I start my day so that I can listen to my soul, hear God's messages for me, and share my heart with him.

Next, I make an effort on a daily basis to do someone a good turn without their knowledge. If they find out, it doesn't count. Also, I do two things I don't want to do, just for exercise. These are usually making my bed and doing the dishes. Grow a thicker skin! Today, I will not show anyone that my feelings are hurt. They may be hurt, but today, I will not show it.

Lastly, I will be agreeable. I will look as well as I can.

I will dress and comb my hair. Maybe put on some lipstick. I will keep my voice low and I will not criticize one bit. I practice the three C's: Do not criticize, condemn, or complain. I will try not to regulate anyone but myself. God has created each person in his image. We do not know what is best for others. We can just accept that there are no mistakes and we can bless the person, place, or situation. We can look to see how we can change ourselves to be more loving and accepting, and we can pray for their best.

We need to find a program that works for us. Whether this is found in an exercise group, a church group, a yoga group, or a meditation group, all of it works. I chose a 12-step food program. It worked for me because there were guidelines, parameters, and boundaries. There was a HOW (Honesty, Open-mindedness, and Willingness) and a fellowship of like-minded people. There was support. There was accountability. There were ways to measure the growth. There was encouragement. It is a portable program that I can take with me every day, everywhere I go. I can work on myself and become a better person.

Find what works for you!

Don't let perfectionism derail you! I don't do this program perfectly. After three years of back-to-back abstinence, I lost my abstinence.

After moving to the desert when COVID hit and being alone for so long, far from my support system, I realized that there was no one to keep me accountable. There were no meetings in my city. No one saw me. I was not going to any of my regular twelve-step meetings. It was up to me whether I used a tool or not. It was easy to hide out. Although I had lost my weight and was in a healthy body, I still had a lot of inner work to do. So, when loneliness or worry or fear hit, I would soothe myself with food.

After two years of abstinence (no flour, sugar, or alcohol), I gave in and began buying chips and candy. I started with sugar-free. I told myself it didn't count because it was not sugar. However, it also was not what I had committed to on my food plan. It was not weighed and measured. It was true when the founders of my food program said, "An open bag is an empty bag." Once I started, I literally could not stop. This new practice became a habit and set up cravings.

Before I knew it, I was back into the addiction and kept repeating this process every time I went to a gas station. I would go inside and buy chips and candy and I would finish them in the car. As soon as it was gone I wanted more. Food addiction is progressive. The one bag led to two, and just like the cocaine 30 years earlier, I needed more and more to satisfy the addiction. I could not believe that I had slipped back into this terrible addiction. I was once again hurting myself with food. Why? I guess I was failing to look at the feelings inside that were trying to come up. Was I hungry? No. Was I angry? No. Was I Lonely? Yes. Was I tired? Yes! ... HALT. When we are Hungry, Angry, Lonely, or Tired, we need to take a HALT—a pause. In these times, we need to take a time-out and do nothing.

Nothing except go within. Pray and nurture ourselves. Ask God for guidance. PAUSE and ask to be directed. Pause Action Until Serenity Enters, and only then move forward.

"HALT"

This morning, I was thinking about how this slogan has affected my life.

My 12-step program says that we need to practice self-care and HALT…don't get too Hungry, Angry, Lonely, or Tired.

Hungry: I did not grow up hungry. There was always enough for me to eat. But I realized that if I waited too long to eat and became over-hungry, I would make bad choices.

Angry: As an adolescent I became angry. As a result of my parent's divorce, the rape, and finding out that my father was not my real father, my anger grew and grew. I used the food to push those feelings down.

Lonely: I think this is the one that took me down. As a young child, an only child, my parents both worked and I was left alone a lot. My mother also felt guilty for coming into the marriage with a young child, so when she wasn't working, she was catering to her husband, and that meant they needed their alone time, leaving me alone to entertain myself.

Tired: When I'm tired my program is at risk. If I don't make time to have the food in the house before I commit it to my sponsor, I risk being unprepared when it's time to eat and I might binge. When I'm tired, I know that my resistance is low.

We need to acknowledge that all is well, stay in the day, and take the next right action. We don't try to fix something that is a week, a month, or a year out. We simply look around and say, what is the next right action NOW? Make our bed? Yes! Do the dishes? Yes! Call the client we've been putting off calling? Yes! Once we begin to take those positive actions, we begin to feel better. We can do hard things! All is well. The trick is to take the emotion out of it and do the next right action. Feelings are not facts. It works if you work it, and you're worth it!

CHAPTER 15

Lessons Learned

This is not a self-help book. It is simply my attempt to show you the lessons I've learned along my journey. Self-improvement is something that we continually work on. We don't graduate, we just practice it, and by practicing it, we improve and get better.

If I can turn my negative self-talk around and create a beautiful life, so can you! Of course, my life is a work in progress, but if used, the tools in this book work. We are responsible for our own happiness. I am very grateful to have a life that I love and one that I can sustain for years to come. I can enjoy a sane and happy life in service to others, being a blessing to those who have had similar struggles.

* * * * *

It had been years since I'd thought of that day so long ago when my innocence was stolen.

With my divorce final, and living alone, I had time on my hands. One day I was mindlessly typing in names of people from my past in Las Vegas to see where they had landed.

I entered the name Michael Anderson and was shocked to see an article about him from the The Las Vegas Sun, the newspaper that had brought me so much angst years before. I had buried this memory, along with countless other feelings of shame and pain, that had haunted me for years.

My rapist was released from prison in June 2021 with the distinction of being the longest-serving inmate in Nevada for murder. He served 47 years for the murder of a 22-year-old co-worker. He is now free. I often wonder if he thinks about what he did to me. Did he ever feel remorse? Did his years in prison teach him anything? Did anyone ever rape him while he was there? What were his years like? What is he like now?

I was able to forgive him and be neutral around the assault. He had his own pain and suffering. I learned that his hell started when he got involved in drugs. He was supposed to be watching his younger brother while his parents were at work. Instead, he got high and distracted and his little brother wandered off and fell into the family swimming pool and drowned. Mike's world was never the same. I can feel empathy for his situation and understand that he was trying to cope with his own anger and loss. I can let it go with love.

* * * * *

Take responsibility for your life. I love the saying, "If it's to be, it's up to me!"

I've been clean and sober for over a decade. I've had many trials and tribulations in my life, and I am far from perfect, but I am on a daily path of recovery. Each morning, I wake up glad to be alive, and I have set parameters for how I will live my life. These guidelines keep me sane, serene, and close to God.

Most of everything that is bothering us can be attributed to not living in the present. If we are stressed out and worried about something in the future that we cannot control, and which hasn't happened yet, or if we are regretting the past and replaying old scenarios that can't be changed, we need to change our thinking. The only thing that we can change is the way we look at these occurrences. We can waste time, or we can bless them, and say we did our best with what we had, and we will do better next time. Beyond that, we only have today.

TODAY is what counts.

This memoir is my love letter to myself to say that my life has mattered. I'm grateful for every twist and turn that might have at first looked like a mistake, but now I see it was really a lesson. A lesson to show that I was off course and a gentle nudge as to how and where to get back on the path. Also, to take it a step further, every experience was perfect. Even if it seemed like a mistake or tragedy at the time, it invariably led me to a lesson I needed to learn or to something better.

When I look back and evaluate my life, I can admittedly say there were many less-than-shining moments. Times when I made questionable choices. Selfish choices. But what I've learned is that all things happen for good—either our good or someone else's. God does not make mistakes. It is all part of the bigger plan.

I can look back on my life and see how my choices have brought me to where I am today. I am grateful for all that I have and all that I've done. Everything happened as it was meant to—I have no regrets. As a result, I have a son who, although we do not share any DNA, is a gift from God and I will always cherish our relationship.

Now, no longer a child, I see and better understand the limitations of my family of origin. They did the best they could. My father could not help his lack of emotion or his inability to nurture. He gave what he had been given by his parents and no more. My mother was a child, raising a child. She loved me and yet was limited in her own capacity. I can accept my parents where they were, and I can love and forgive them. I can also love and forgive myself. Looking back, I have no regrets. There is nothing that I would have done differently. Each choice led me to something important in my life that I may not have had if

I had not taken the path before it. I'm on a sacred journey and I'm grateful for all the lessons I've learned along the way.

The universe, God, and our angels are talking to us all day, every day. We just need to be present and use our senses to see, listen, and notice the messages that are gently guiding us.

In his book, *The Power of Now*, Eckhart Tolle, a well-known spiritual teacher, explores presence, thinking, and spirituality. The book explains how our thinking can introduce needless pain and suffering, and how to reduce this in your life by living in the present.

Our minds are so powerful. They are like computers, efficient, and without emotion. If we program them with correct data, they will give us the results we want.

We can achieve great things if we just visualize what we want as though they were already here. The Bible said, "...call those things that be not, as if they were" (Romans 4:17).

It is a two-fold process. One is to know what we want and hold that desire in our mind; the next is to raise our vibration to the level and emotion we want as though we already have it. Feel the feeling. Plug into the excitement about that which you want. Get excited for this moment and express gratitude for what is being given to you. Raise your energy and let God know that you appreciate what he has provided.

Mark 11:24:

"Therefore, I tell you whatever you ask for in prayer, believe that you have it and it will be yours."

I've been following the teachings of Louise Hay since the '80s. She was an American motivational author, professional speaker, and AIDS advocate. She authored several New Thought self-help books, including the 1984 book, *You Can Heal Your Life*, and at age 84 founded Hay House Publishing. She healed her own cancer by visualizing herself well. Each morning I turn on YouTube and listen to Louise Hay and her affirmations as a way to program my mind and weed out negativity.

Each evening before bed, I make a gratitude list. I write down 12 things I am grateful for. I do this each night and read it aloud in the morning.

Here is an example of mine:
I'm grateful for this day.
I'm grateful for my beautiful home.
I'm grateful for my strong body.
I'm grateful for my healthy animals.
I'm grateful for my strong immune system.
I'm grateful for my wonderful curious mind.
I'm grateful that my work is constantly being rewarded.
I'm grateful that my money is always being replenished.
I'm grateful that vast sums of money come to me from various sources on a continuous basis.
I'm grateful that I'm alive and have this beautiful day to create.

Remember to write the things in the present tense as though they have already happened.

Another of my teachers, Abraham, was introduced to us in the '80s by Jerry and Esther Hicks. Abraham is a collective of entities that speak to us through Esther and impart wisdom to us. I love to listen to their teachings on YouTube as they discuss the way to raise our vibration and resonate with joy.

Anytime that I notice my energy is low, I like to stand up tall and raise my arms to the sky and visualize white light coming out of the ground, moving energy into my feet, up through my body, and out my head, and as I visualize a surging stream of white light shooting out of the top of my head I say "I am here, I can do it." I plant my feet strongly on the ground, legs slightly apart, feeling the strong beam of white light shooting upward from the ground through my body and out into the sky. I hold that vision for a moment and then I shake it all off and take the NEXT right action. Continue to take the action even when you are not sure. Just do the thing that takes you closer to the thing you set out to do, keeping the end result in your sight.

When I was going through my divorce, I found it extremely helpful to listen to Joel Osteen, as he recited the scriptures of God's promises. His teachings encouraged us to say these promises out loud and remind him.

"God, you said your plan is to prosper us (Jeremiah 29:11), so God, cause me to prosper according to your word. Thank you for the people that you have assigned to bless my life financially. Bless them even more abundantly for their obedience. Amen."

"God, you said I would lend and not borrow (Deuteronomy 15:6)..."

* * * * *

Two of the most valuable and important lessons that have helped me are the ACCEPTANCE paragraph and the RESENTMENT paragraph in the *Big Book of Alcoholics Anonymous*. These have been told by others but they are key if we are going to grow.

Acceptance, from the *Big Book of Alcoholics Anonymous*: "Acceptance is the answer to all my problems today. When I am disturbed, it is because I find some person, place, thing, or situation—some fact of my life—unacceptable to me and I can find no serenity until I accept that person, place, thing, or situation as being exactly the way it is supposed to be at this moment.

"I need to accept that everything in my life is exactly as it is supposed to be at this moment. Nothing happens in God's world by mistake."

When we complain about a person or a situation, we are criticizing God's handiwork. We are saying that we know better than God. We need a new set of glasses. Focus on the good and you will see more of it.

The *Big Book* says that we can not afford to hold onto resentment. Resentment is the number one offender that can keep us from our joy.

If you find yourself struggling to let go of resentment, here are some other things to try:

- **Explore the feelings behind your resentment.** What's the first thing that comes to mind when you think of the incident that caused you to resent the person? Embarrassment or shame? Inadequacy? Fear? In most cases, it's not that the person did something unforgivable, but that they made you feel a way that you really didn't like, which was channeled into anger to protect your wounded ego.

- **Be empathetic**. Make a genuine effort to try and see things from their point of view and ignore what your intentions were or any other information that they could not have known. Considering their actions through a different lens can help you realize that the situation may not have been as black and white as you previously thought. Misunderstandings happen.

- **Focus on gratitude.** Considering the positive things in your life can provide some much-needed perspective. In the grand scheme of things, a quarrel with a friend or romantic partner might not be the big deal you initially thought it was.

- **Bonus:** Positive thinking can lower your stress, which can make it easier for you to let go of those negative feelings.

It can be challenging to work through resentment alone. Find a person you trust, such as a therapist, coach, or AA sponsor to talk through your feelings with. Having a neutral third party to consult can help you navigate your emotional blind spots.

These lessons are available to all of us and have been around since the beginning of time. We need only to put them into practice. Just like a yoga practice, piano practice, or basketball practice, this is mental practice. We must train our minds to think positively and be grateful for everything we have right now. Without the promises of anything else coming. When we can accept and appreciate that what we have today is enough, miracles will happen. We must be completely satisfied right now and then we will get more and more and more!

* * * * *

As Les Brown likes to say, "To fulfill my destiny, I need to be around lifters and thrusters…not weights and drags."

Resist perfectionism: When we are being perfectionists, we are criticizing our creativity. We must allow all of our ideas to come out and flow. Once we have set all of our ideas free, we can go back and edit these ideas. We can eliminate the fluff or the flowery or the excess that doesn't add value. Once we take away the excess, the beauty of what we are trying to create comes forth. It shows itself.

Edit your life: Clear the clutter! In addition to having a mental and emotional program, we need to have the right space to create our new life. Order is very important in our lives and minds. When we want to take on a project and/or begin our day and our work area is filled with clutter, our mind is in chaos. We must clean things up before we begin and clear our workspace so that our thoughts and ideas can come through clearly. Having a blank canvas makes us feel calmer, and we are less stressed out when we are not looking at the stacks of things that need to be done.

Of all the lessons learned, the biggest takeaway for me is that gratitude is everything. Having a loving and grateful heart keeps us free from resentment. We are owed nothing. When we know that we are owed nothing, we understand that everything we have or don't have is a gift. A gift that we can be grateful for. That sense of appreciation raises our vibration and draws more good to come to us. It is like a magnet. The universe wants to grant us all of our wishes and desires. If we understand this concept, we can deliberately construct and live our best life.

When I moved to the desert, I did not know that I would fall in love with the land. Each day as I spent time alone with it, I began to know its personality. Each change spoke to me and I noticed. When a blade of grass would poke its head through the barren sand and say, "Hey look at me—I am here," I would applaud and celebrate it. Each time I found something buried that had been here for years, I would dig it out, dust it off, and invariably find a purpose for it in today's time and place, which delighted me. I also felt connected to the former owner who had loved this land and built all of the structures here.

Thank you for this day, Lord. Please guide my thoughts, words, and deeds. Show me your will for me. I am open. I am listening. Thank you for a chance to show up today and see this beautiful life you have in store for me.

I am blessed and highly favored. I'd adopted this mantra years before when a friend of mine demonstrated the technique to me when she was going through treatment for cancer which she cured on her own with God's help. Anytime I asked,

"How are you?" my voice heavy with sympathy, sure that she had been beaten and death was imminent, wanting to hear every gory detail of her health situation, she would reply strongly, confidently, and clearly,

"I am blessed and highly favored."

Ok, I would think to myself and smile. Let's do that. Let's get on board with the faith that God can do anything. He (or she) is God after all.

I am a child of God. I deserve love and the best the universe has to offer me.

I have all that I need and I'm so grateful. My bank account continues to multiply. My health is excellent. My stomach is full. My animals are healthy and happy. All is well and I am glad. Today, I will continue to clear the clutter so that what I have represents my life today. Today, I will be fully present. Today, I will be grateful. I will move my body and make sure that it is strong. I will do my best for my clients. I am alive and I will resonate with joy and possibility. Thank you, Lord. Only good lies before me. I am prosperous.

Writing this book has been a dream of mine for years. I'm so grateful to have completed this work with the support and instruction of those I admire so much. I want to give back and help others. I want to motivate and cheer others on. My goal is to help others realize that it is never too late to achieve all they desire if they just believe and take the next right action.

The journey to completing this book was long and challenging. Often, I would stop and tell myself that my story didn't matter—that it was not interesting or unique. Plus, I was reluctant to share my shameful experiences with you or show myself in a bad light.

But what I came to learn in reading Viktor Frankl's *Man's Search for Meaning* was that we must make peace with our past. We must own it and yet start with a clean slate every day. My past experiences have made me who I am today and the events that happened made me stronger and more resilient.

I am proud of who I am and who I've become. I am learning to love myself unconditionally. I am learning to measure my wins by the progress I've made, not the ideals that I've set for myself. I am a work in progress and I'm grateful for each day that I am here with the opportunity to keep learning and growing.

I've created a life that offers me freedom. I can afford my lifestyle and I can work from anywhere in the world and travel.

All is possible if you believe. As my dear friend Marina said, "All is well in the end, and if it's not well, it is not the end." Keep reaching for your joy every day and do what you came here to do. You are a gift. Stay in the present.

About the Author

Deborah Collins was raised in Las Vegas and relocated to Los Angeles to pursue her love of real estate and became a real estate paralegal. After working in-house with many Fortune 500 companies, she started her own company in 1995 representing retail tenants and landlords in their real estate needs. She married and began flipping houses and during one of those projects acquired two horses and began a lifelong love of all things equestrian.

Deborah is now a Business and Life Coach trained in the NLP Method.

She lives with her three horses, three chickens, and two dogs in a small community in Kern County, California, where she loves to ride and commune with her animals. Her other interests include golf and travel.

www.ingramcontent.com/pod-product-compliance
Lightning Source LLC
Chambersburg PA
CBHW070914120626
46546CB00001B/263